The Way It Was

..and That

Recollections.. from old Mayo

by Joe Coen

Copyright © 2020 by Joe Coen.

THE WAY IT WAS - AND THAT

ISBN: 978-1-906628-680

Published by CheckPoint Press, Ireland.

CheckPoint
Press

www.checkpointpress.com

The Way It Was ..and That

Recollections of old Mayo

by Joe Coen

Contents

The area of East and North-East County Mayo as covered in this book.

Aghamore is South-East of the centre of the area shown.

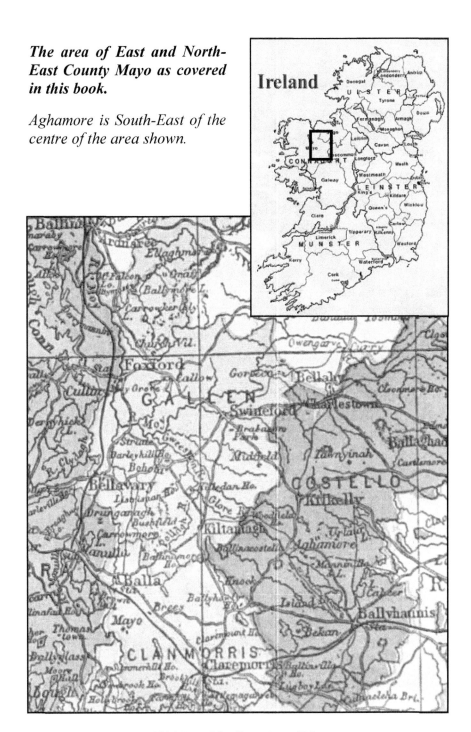

Old Map of the Baronies of Mayo

Introduction

MY FIRST EXPERIENCE of transport that I can remember is on horse-back. I'd be put astride one of the horses as they were led to the fields for ploughing. I used to hold on to the tops of the hames[1] as the ground was swept from under me. After a while I was able to relax a little so that I could look around me from this great height. Sometimes I would smile back to the people who waved at me as we passed in what was almost a ceremonial procession.

Later I learnt how to ride the ass, and the fall off his back was not so dangerous as would be a fall off a horse, but my falls off the ass were frequent. When I became accustomed to being a jockey on the ass, I used to urge him to speeds that were beyond his preferred limits, and, so he objected. He devised a scheme. Suddenly and without warning he would apply his brakes, and at the same time lower his head, so that the jockey sailed over his ears and landed five or six yards in front of him. Apparently satisfied that he had effectively cancelled any further racing at least for that evening, he would resume his search for good grazing.

Soon I grew tired of ass riding, and the next aspiration that I had was to try to ride a bicycle. You had to rely totally on your power to propel the bicycle, but at least it would not play tricks on you like the ass.

Most of the grown-ups in my time had learnt how to ride a bicycle, and so bicycles were fairly plentiful. However the period of which I speak was during the Second World War years, and so bicycles and parts for them became scarce and most

---

[1] 'Hames': two curved pieces of iron or wood attached to the collar of a draught horse, to which the traces are attached.

expensive. Those who had wealth could always find a good bicycle to buy, but the poor had to improvise. I remember seeing bicycles parked outside the church with pedals made of a square piece of wood. Tyres too had to be invented to match the new circumstance. Sometimes little discs of old tyres were strung together with wire rather like a string of daisies, and these, when fitted on the bicycle wheels, acted as solid tyres. Others used to twist a rope of hay and wrap it around the rim of the wheels and then fit an old tyre on over the hay rope.

Somehow we all learnt how to ride a bicycle,and the burning ambition of most young people was to have a bicycle of their own. The first bicycle that I owned was a fairly basic model. It had two good wheels and a new chain, and one good brake. Extravagances like handgrips or carriers were not essential. Later I graduated to a bicycle with a three-speed gear and a hub dynamo.

Very soon the days of the bicycle were over. Bright colours or even five-speed gears did not satisfy. The bicycles were abandoned under the hedges to rot away and everybody aspired to have at least one motor car in the household. I must admit that like the rest of men I too succumed to the craze of the motor car.

For years I was content like most to sit motionless behind the wheel of a motor car. It began to dawn on me that here I was sitting like a zombie, and that unless I took some action soon I would become a zombie. To regain a little of my youthful vigor I felt that I needed some form of movement. My footballing days were over, and running was never something that I enjoyed. Then I remembered the days of long ago when I used to enjoy cycling.

I found that bicycles have been improved upon since I first began to cycle. A modern electric bicycle for examle, seems to take much of the hardship out of cycling. With the electric bicycle you just pedal along as you would do on an ordinary bicycle, but to assist you going into a headwind or up an incline, you just flick on a switch, and the road seems to level out, or, the wind does not really reach you any more.

I tried out my new machine, and I faced into fairly steep hills, and I reached to the top. As for the wind, I always remembered that whatever way you face on a bicycle the wind seems to be in your face. However I feel sure that once I catch a sight of the blue peak of Cruagh Padraig and the round hulk of Neifin Mor, like Raftery of old, "go m'bein aris og!" - I'd be young again!

It is donkey's years since I pedalled around Aghamore. But what am I saying? A donkey never lived so long! To maintain a proper atmosphere in my tours recorded in this journal, I hope to start each journey from Bruff, which was my old stamping ground.

I wrote these pieces simply to put on record a little about my adult neighbours whom I knew well when I was growing up. I have no other agenda. I have to be honest and put down these activities as I remember them. Others may look back and see things differently. The one thing I want to avoid is to cast any aspertions on the fine people who were all my friends.

1

Leaving The Nest

THE GREEN UNDULATING landscape around where I grew up had so many mysteries for a boy to explore. In summer time when the ash and the sycamore and the hawthorn were in bloom in their summer finery they extended an invitation that needed to be fully explored. There were clumps of hazel and blackthorn that we called "closhes" and the variety of the fruits of these trees were well known to me. The older people could take a hazel nut or two, but they would never make a feast of them. Sloes—the fruit of the blackthorn—were lumped all together as 'bitter' and were just tasted, and then spat out. We, the younger folk, knew the secret places where sweet sloes grew.

In my growing-up days I was limited in my exploration by not having a boy of near to my own age with whom I could explore. I did have a sister a little bit older than myself and she could substitute in most cases. Generally speaking girls do not seem to enjoy tree climbing as much as boys. They also mature more quickly than boys, and often prevent the development of activities, by threatening to tell at home. In some cases they would be the first to plead their case in such a way as to shift the onus of proof on to their male accomplices.

I was however very lucky in my growing days, that nearby there was a white-haired man with a big white moustache. He was long past the age for drawing the old–age pension, but beneath that weather-beaten old face beat the heart of a young boy. He knew where the worms could be found that would tempt the red-gulled perches in the lake. He had studied the ways of the wild song birds and he was always willing to share this information with those who had an interest in such matters.

He told me of how he had at one time found a blackbird's nest low down on a furze bush out in a field. He happened to have made a bird cage about twice as big as an ordinary cage. He hung this cage beside the blackbird's nest. In a few days he moved the cage right up to the nest, and when the chicks were out of the shell he put the nest and the little birds into the cage. The adult birds fed their chicks through the wire of the cage. Little by little he moved the cage until he hung it high up on the back wall of his house.

The exciting part came when the yellow-billed male blackbird came and perched on top of the cage and whistled his melodies. This became an evening performance just as the sun was setting behind the blue-coloured mountains. At this point he would put the family cat in close house-arrest and then opened the door of the cage. The plan was to select a male bird and confine him to the cage. The problem was that all of the young looked alike, but he selected one which he chanced might have a yellow bill. For a few days he watched the little bird all alone in the cage and he seemed to be so sad. The whole clutch used to come occasionally and look at their one family member in confinement. My friend became so sorry for the poor fellow in confinement that one day he opened the cage door and let the last one out. For years afterwards blackbirds used to come and perch on top of the cage and whistle for all that they were worth.

I remember once when my friend advised me how to make a trap to catch a live hare. My father was complicit in this scheme, for hares had practically demolished a plot of cabbage plants which he had, by hard work with a spade, dug and cultivated in a corner of bog. The plan was to dig a hole about three feet deep and then to make the bottom of the hole much wider than the neck at the top. You covered this hole over with light material in such a way that the hare would not suspect that it was unsafe ground. We had done such a good job in the camouflage that the unfortunate hare was trapped. I was very excited when I saw that the trap had been sprung. I could hear the animal splashing about the water for the hole had half filled with water.

The poor fellow was all wet and as he tried to gain purchase on the soft ground he apparently fell back on his back. I procured a stout stick and I was intent on striking the creature on the head. However when I went up close to him, he stood still and he began to cry just

like a child. Each time when I went close up to him he started this cry. There was nobody about and so I threw a few sods of turf down into the hole and then the hare sprang clear up out of the hole. I watched as he almost flew down the bog away from me. Then he stopped and looked back for a few moments and then he slinked away, as they do. This was not the sort of a story that a man would tell to his pals, certainly not pals of his own age. Some of the hare's descendants are still lurking around the same area so very many years later.

I remember one harvest morning I saw my friend outside our gate. He had his big horse with him and the horse was fully dressed in the tacklings for the cart, but he was not yoked to the cart. This was a bit odd. To stand outside our gate was also strange, for he would normally come right into the house shouting and laughing as he approached. Now he just stood there and I saw my father come out of the house with one side of his face shaved and the white lather on the other side of his face. They spoke in a low voice, which I could not hear clearly. To interrupt father at his weekly shave was extraordinary, for this was an operation at which he never allowed any interruptions.

I watched my old friend go back out our road leading his horse; he disappeared from my view around the back of his house. A few minutes later I saw two cars coming up the main road and they both pulled into my friend's house. This was getting exciting, and I was about to go out to investigate (for motor cars were rarely seen in our parts) but my father—now fully shaved—dissuaded me and he walked quickly out the road. The next thing I saw was another car coming down the road and it also stopped beside the other two cars. I knew that the car and the big man in the dark suit and glasses was the Parish Priest.

I found a seat on top of a high sod fence from which I could have a good view. I saw two or three big men standing about the cars and I could see my friend's white head amongst them. They got into the small blue car that I had first seen coming up the road. This car turned up the road. I could see the square back on the car and the spare wheel with the spokes painted red. It moved off slowly at first. I could see the tail of blue smoke that followed this car. This tail of smoke seemed to hang on to the back of the car and it grew wider as it rose up into the air and it lingered there after the car had gone. Most of all I remember the sad lonely moaning sound the car made like some wild creature from far away. The sound stopped and then resumed again with an even louder and more piercing noise that lingered on long after the car had gone out of sight, and even after the blue smoke had disappeared into the air.

With the wisdom acquired over the years I now know that this break in the sound was when the driver pressed in the clutch to change gears. Equally I now know that this sound to me that sounded so strange was no more than a reflection of the urgency which was felt by the driver and his two passengers, who were escorting my kindly neighbour away to a place where his freedom would be restricted. The sound of the engine of this car long ago is not so out of place in today's extensive use of motor cars. Yet whenever or wherever I hear an engine being pushed to its limits, I am reminded of that harvest day so long ago.

I had not been given any information, but from close observation I had deduced that some sad and very serious business was going on. Our dog Bran seemed also to sense that I needed some companionship and he came up and sat beside me on top of the fence. The tears filled my eyes, and I did not wish to seen crying like a "girleen" so I wandered up the fields until my eyes had dried.

In a few months my friend had returned home and before long he was back again observing the wonders of nature, and almost daily he had new stories of what he had seen and heard. He always retained his great gift of being able to communicate with people of all ages.

2

My Early Education

I PEDALLED OUT THE narrow little road out to the N17 and I turned left up towards the Knock Shrine. Traffic was sweeping up and down with little notice taken of the lone cyclist on his spanking-new electric bicycle. I dismounted at the crossroads and the memories of many years skipped through my mind. I once knew every stone that stood around this crossroads, and I know that when I sit down these memories will come floating back to me. It was here at this scene that I received my early social education. This was our social-centre but we did not use this name at the time. The name for such places was an innovation that was to be invented many years later. This was the place where I completed my education. In other words this was my finishing school.

The scene that first comes to me is of a Sunday evening, a game of handball in progress. The ball is played up against the side wall of the granary, where it hops back onto the surface of the tarred road. I can see the tall dark-haired young man as he stands motionless as if dozing off to sleep, and then, when the ball comes his way he springs  into action sending the ball about an inch above the tarmac so that it rebounds out along the ground. A cheer rises from the crowd of onlookers. The other player, a small man, stands with both hands out ready to strike, and his big wild eyes are dancing in his head. He strikes the ball in such a way that it comes out high, but the tall man reaches up his hand and again strikes it low towards the wall.

The small man has a look of anger about him, and when traffic gathers on each side of the players he keeps on playing, but the tall man finally grabs the ball and he smiles at the road users and swings his arm to invite them to pass on. The traffic at that time consisted mostly of bicycles and a few motor cars. There are many spectators, some just leaning on their bicycles and others sitting on the loose stone wall. There is another group of younger men standing around the entrance to the cart-house.

Some have flashlamps fitted on their bicycles and many too have overcoats rolled up and held in position by the spring carrier on their bicycles. Suddenly, a wild cheer rises up from the crowd as all heads turn towards a very tall, slightly-built fair-haired young man whose face reddens right up to the hair line on his forehead. He shows a broad smile, but looks as if he would willingly disappear underground if such a facility were available. He was wheeling a lady's bicycle, which was not made or intended for such a long-legged man. This tall shy youth had apparently tried to steal quietly in amongst the crowd without attracting any notice.

I remember seeing a man with white hair and deep lines stretching from his eyes down to his chin. He was at least old enough to have been the boy's father, and he was actively engaged in drawing attention to the unfortunate young man. Later on I discovered that this man had made his reputation as a local wit by drawing attention to defenceless people who were unlikely to ever attempt to try to return the favour. Perhaps this was part of the "Clar oibre" which is the kind of expression we used long ago. However, this tall youth became strong, and just once he resorted to physical force and the word got out. Nobody ever attempted to turn a laugh on him again. A remedy still used in the most sophisticated of societies.

Further down the road about fifty yards on the right hand side was the sod fence over which we used to climb into the "sraith mor" where we used to play football on a Sunday after Mass. I looked over the fence and in amongst the rushes which have grown profusely in recent years. After a little concentration I spotted the great brown stone barely peering through the ground which served as one goal post, and the first jacket to be taken off made the second goal post. We never had a second set of goal posts, for two or three men lined the goal mouth to kick out the ball amongst the main group of participants, and whomsoever got the ball tried to kick the ball high into the goal mouth. If the ball went beyond the reach of the goalies there were a few young boys who would fight for the ball to have their kick from the back of the goals. To prepare for the game you simply took off your jacket and pulled your socks up outside your trousers legs.

On the opposite side of the road and a little farther on was the "Cluain"[1] where Michael, a local worker. He also sometimes worked as a farmer. Some local people were known simply by their first name. His neighbour Gerry was also known by his first name. I think this identification by first names only, was a sign of the prestige in which these men were held.

Michael was a reluctant farmer, and I think that he much preferred to be working at his trade, which included all manner of work with timber including house building. I recall that there was once growing in what was known as the apple field, a tall willow. It grew as tall as an ash tree, and then one winter a great wind came and blew down the tall willow. Michael a resourceful man could see in the carcass of the tree an opportunity for an enterprise. The period was during the Second World War, and materials of all sorts were often unobtainable. Boots and shoes were very scarce and so Michael set about sawing up the old willow and his carpenter's skills enabled him to make clog soles. The wood of the willow is very lightweight and so he used to cut off the worn leather soles from old boots and shoes and attach the new wooden soles, thus giving a second life to old boots and shoes.

 The crude clog-irons were much like miniature horse shoes and they were very expensive. Some resourceful people at that time used to make clog-irons out of the handles off buckets, and these were more agricultural than the

[1] "Cluain": the name of a weed which grew profusely in this field.

originals. Michael used to cut off a little piece from a bicycle tyre and nail these on to the newly-fashioned clogs. In those times it was not unusual to find footprints on soft ground with the following: "Dunlop 28 x 1 and a half. "

Sometimes, in the course of his work if Michael came across a piece of ash timber with a suitable grain he would cut out a dozen hurleys. Many men of his age came strongly under the influence of the old Sinn Fein and so he used to try to make hurlers out of his own sons and those of his neighbours, and thus fashion them into real Irishmen. We would move into any convenient field and there was never any complaint. The bespectacled postman was another neighbour who was keen on all kinds of sport and he never had any objection if we decided to move into his field to play hurling. Our standard of performance was below par, and we used often tell Michael that he should make hurleys with bigger heads.

Hurling never became very popular with us for many had no hurley, and had to improvise; one might use a piece of a board or a walking stick with the hand side turned towards the ground. I remember another man named Michael who used to sometimes join us. He was older than the rest of us and he used to take his place around the goalmouth. On one occasion he could not find either a hurley or even a stick, so he took a short shovel and he played with this. He could pick up the ball easily, but his puck-out was a bit uncertain. However, he was a great deterrent to keep the forwards well out, for there were none willing to face the vicious shovel. I think that we provided a high level of satisfaction from the spectator's point of view. At the first few shouts of our game, a stately looking middle-aged man used to come over the narrow road to see for himself. I can see him still with his tweed cap placed with careful accuracy on his great head. Years later when I used to see the late President De Valera at fairly close up; I was always reminded of the tall spectator who used to come to enjoy our hurling. Each had had exactly the same air of mystique about them.

I felt that these grand people were very close to me as I moved off again slowly up the road to another centre of excellence at the junction of the Curhavnagh (the name of the townsand) road with

the N17. This was the place where a fairly select group used to play pitch and toss. The "spud"—which was a stone about the size of a big potato—was placed on the centre of the minor road. At about ten paces backward the pitcher stood and threw pennies as close as he could to the spud. Each player in turn did likewise and the closest to the spud won the first toss. Most young men with hair in those days used to carry a comb in their pocket, and so three or four pennies were placed on the comb and they were tossed into the air. The winnings were those pennies that fell, heads up. Sometimes the postman and others of the moneyed classes used to make a side bet on the results of the toss.

The next centre of excitement along my route was Cruach a Bhaine, which was a steep hill. This too provided some excitement, for if you got the bike going well with a few extra rounds of the pedals and you reached the top, you could, on the way down, reach speeds unmeasured in those days. It was recorded that a few very powerful men had cycled up this hill and their feat was witnessed by credible witnesses. However, the cost of replacing the bicycle chain was a consideration that prevented me from ever trying this feat. The donkey would happily trot off down the hill with the cart pushing him, but coming up he relied upon human help to bring the cart to the summit. The new N17 seems to be not nearly as steep. These modern road builders do spoil all the fun out of travelling.

I hesitated for a moment, before releasing my bicycle to gain whatever speed it would, for I could see the climb that lay all the way up past the large yellow building that was once O'Brien's shop. I could never pass the Meeltrane Bridge without stopping to look into the clear silver water. I always hoped that I might spot a fish. This bridge has lost a lot of its majesty since the road-makers got at it. I looked eastwards and I noted the small fields sloping northwards towards the river. It was on this land that my maternal grandfather Tom Boyle grew up into a man big enough to go to England to earn a living. The last members of the family have died out and there were no replacements.

My sister and brother and one other are all that is living in Ireland of the once prolific Boyle breed that roamed around these parts. The farm had become enlarged and it was a viable holding. It was a holding of land that might have supported a family, but the change was too late. Lone bachelors would just lurk about, visiting pubs waiting and searching for a mate, but the girls could not wait and now are probably the mothers of children in some town in industrial England.

The Meeltrane Crossroads is another centre where for generations the young male members of the communities from the adjacent town lands, used to congregate. Like so many centres of its kind, this is now deserted at all times. I used to walk along this route to school when I was six years of age. I had a habit of investigating whatever I met with along the sides of the road for I was never in a great hurry to reach school. However I could tell by the cackling of John Freeley's hens if it was time to hurry on to school. I supposed that most hens behaved in the same manner and followed the same timetable.

I used to walk smartly up past the O'Brien's who were building a new house and shop. A visit to this spot and the bakery where they used to make loaves would have to wait until my return journey. I would hurry past Carney's who kept a male pig. All of the activities at his centre were carried out behind closed doors, but details were of much speculation to our group in school.

The schoolmaster lived a little closer to the school. He had previously taught in a school a few miles away, and when he was appointed to the local school the boys continued to refer to him as 'Jim' as was the custom in the locality. However in the case of a school master it was unacceptable to have the children refer to their teacher as "Jim". This air of familiarity did not lead to good discipline either. Jim could not so well be seen going into school in the morning carrying a bundle of canes, for fear that some of the adult population might be making jokes about the means of motivation being used by the local esteemed teacher. Finally in desperation, Jim left the school by the back door one day, and went across the fields to where he knew willows grew profusely and soon returned with an armful of young willow rods.

"Ye are not afraid of me, but I will soon bleddy-well make ye afraid!"

With that statement he proceeded to pull off the leaves and prepare the willows for use. He got his message across without ever having to use the willows. His pupils learned to respect Jim for the gentle intellectual that he was.

Sometimes Jim would visit the local shop for a chat with any of the variety of customers or others who might call. If Mr O'Brien the proprietor had any reason to leave his shop he might ask Jim to hold on until he returned. In this way Jim became known as, perhaps, a derelict relative of the owner. As a result, commercial travellers and van drivers and other similar intellectuals treated Jim as a person of little consequence.

Jim played up to this image and used to enjoy leading these people into arguments on school subjects such as history or geography. Well into a debate, Jim would proceed to lecture in the manner of the gifted teacher, and then smile wryly to himself at his conquest. He liked to play the role of the village schoolmaster and never had to resort to stylish arrangements to assist him.

I climbed up the steps to the beautiful little church across from the school. It is still as delightful as I remember it. It was here that I made my first confession. In fact, I made quite a few 'first confessions'. Miss Judge used to lead us from the school down to the church. She

would go into the confessional box and we would go into the penitent's side and begin a confession. She would pull aside the curtain and we'd have to say "Bless me Father" and so on. It was much less of an ordeal when eventually we had to face Fr. Loftus.

I walked up the next Sunday with my mother and I received my first holy communion. We had no celebrations, but I remember that I felt very grown up with an air of responsibility. We often called into the church and dipped our hands in the wooden barrel of holy water that was available in the church. I have never forgotten the promises that I made to God on that first occasion when I got communion. Sometimes I have not kept my promises, but He has been good to me always.

3

Riding Into The West

ON THIS DAY, I swing right at Costello's Well at Bruff and I face westwards towards Kiltimagh. The old football field is on my right. I remember the short green grass that used to grow there. Now it is overgrown with rushes, which give it for me a look of desolation. Mick Neary used to make it available to the local G.A.A. club at a very reasonable fee. It was associated with games over a great many years. People from the local towns and villages used to refer to it as, "The Field at Bruff". In fact itis in the townland of Doogarry,This was the official field for playing football, but any garden or field where a football was available was used. In this venue however the players usually wore proper coloured jerseys asssociated with their club. Football boots were almost compulsary, although occasionally you'd see a man playing with wellingtons or hob-nailed boots.

In this field we had some good sports meetings, where long-jump and high-jump and running and cycling—including slow-cycling—which was not so simple, for if you tried to go too slow there was a possibility of falling off, which disqualified a rider. There was one disadvantage to the Bruff field in that it was too close to the road, so spectators could see the events from the roadside without paying the entrance fee. I passed on by the field and I free-wheeled down the little hill coming to Heneghan's Avenue.

The Heneghan family no longer live there, and I noted an auctioneer's notice up on the entrance. The little road leading up to the house is smooth and level very much unlike what it used to be. Many years ago Mickey Heneghan and I used to go to work and we were expected to be there at eight o'clock. Mickey was the proud owner of a very old 'Baby Ford' car which was small, but I can testify that it was by no means light. I think that it had somehuman qualities one of which was laziness. It never would start so early in the morning, but if you could wait until about mid-day it was willing to go.

The convential remedy for lazy motor cars in those days was to push it along for a while and the pilot operated some levers which were supposed to start up the machine. On many a cold winter morning I warmed myself pushing this little car down the rough cobbled road. Invariably it did not start, and so I pushed it along the Cahir road past Johnnie Rogers' old house and then it would send out signals of blue smoke that could be seen as far away as Lismegan. I remember that by this time the sun would be lighting up the road behind us, and so we would steam into the sleeping town of Kiltimagh always just in the neck of time.

There is a pull on the electric bicycle as I go slowly past Ceilia Hosty's house. It was once one of the very few slated houses and now it has just held on to a few slates. I heard it said by the old people that the occupants of this house were related to the people who owned the Coogue Farm. They were Protestants, but they used to have the local priest in there to say Mass when times were tough. Just a short distance past the entrance to this house there is a small white cross to mark the spot where P. D. Kenny steered his bicycle into the side of the road and died still sitting on his bicycle. I remember the evening well. Mick Frain was crossing our bog and had the news for my father. Mr Kenny was highly esteemed by the local community. I remember that my father seemed to be sincerely grieved. I had seen Mr Kenny myself on one occasion, he had a long white beard, and cycled along very slowly.

P.D. Kenny

Mr Kenny was reared in Lismegansion like the rest of his small-farming neighbours. From an early age he showed an interest in learning. He went to England to work when he was sixteen years of age. He was small in frame – indeed he never grew to be very big. He got a job working for a market gardener for some years and then he went on full-time study, and it used to be said that he had a university degree in economics. I never saw any confirmation of this, but he became an editor of a paper in Scotland, and later on, on the recommendations of George Moore, another illustrious Mayoman, Mr Kenny got a job as an art critic with an important newspaper. Mr Moore was a landlord from Claremorris, but he became a nationalist and had great respect for the Irish language, although he never spoke Irish himself. He did however, put a provision in his will that those of his relatives who could not speak Irish would not benefit.

It appears that P.D. Kenny could speak some Irish, because when there was a protest about Synge's play being put on in Dublin, Mr Yeats got P.D. Kenny to speak to the people of Mayo in their own language, and they were appeased and went home peacefully. I suppose that P.D. could drop his acquired upper-class English accent and revert to the local accent, which would be understood by Mayo men. The upper-class Dublin people seem to have been much impressed by Synge's rendering of the Mayo accent.

I remember on one occasion I was giving evidence in the High Court in Dublin, and I described the weather as being "a misty day". The learned lawmen were puzzled as to what I meant until finally in their clipped, upper-class way they concluded that I meant that it was raining lightly. One then mentioned, "the mist that do be on the bog" - a phrase from Synge's play. The Barristers joined the learned Judge in a dignified laugh, in their upper-class way.

Before he went to England he was known as Pateen Patch, but when he returned after about twenty years he was a gentleman known as 'P.D. Kenny'. As Pateen, he seemed to have been on friendly terms with the father of the land league, Michael Davitt, but he never showed the kind of nationalistic fevour of Davitt. Nevertheless Mr Kenny left a highly-paid and prestigous position as an editor of a newspaper, and came home to take over a small and wet little farm. His objective seems to have been to show the Irish how to farm profitably. His writings seemed to be aimed at showing the English how stupid we were, as if he himself were not one of us. I suppose that aim was to improve his sales in England. The English, like the rest of us respond to flattery. In the end he was as impovrished as any of his neighbours.

From here on for at least a half a mile the going is smooth until you come around to Maura Aiteann's. Maura was a member of the Kenny clan whose husband died during the famine, and to sustain herself she set up a butchering business. She had no family, and her dwelling fell away, and the Co Council chopped down the last of the furze bushes so that "Maura of the furze" is meaningless. Few local people now can identify the place. On the opposite side of the road is the little farm made famous by P.D. Kenny. The fine trees still remain to remind the passer-by of his existence. The old landmark Tom Nixon's shop is also closed up. I stopped and looked up the little road with the two high sod fences, and just over the bridge on the little river stands the dwelling and workshop of the late Sonny Leetch. Sonny worked in the kitchen or, more correctly, he was sprawled about the kitchen. His benches and leather and footwear some half-made and others needing repair,were always strewn untidily about the floor. His mother Baby sat on a low stool close to the fire, and they kept up a cheerful banter between them.

Despite the modest surroundings they were both people of great dignity. It may have been that Mrs Leetch's people were at some time evicted out of their home, and despite their intermittent impovrishment they always maintained a high degree of dignity. Sonny worked long days, and was highly skilled in his craft, but on occasions he would have to go to George Delaney's in Ballyhaunis for leather and other items such as heel ball. On such occasions Sonny was known to have indulged in a few drinks, which would develop his natural wit.

The last time I visited his workshop was to have studs hammered into two new pairs of boots. The boots were of a kind that retired schoolmasters might wear or could be often seen on an old Parish Priest. A young fellow—such as I was then—to be getting two pairs of such boots and then getting studs fitted on them, required an explanation. I had to confide in Sonny that I had been called to the Garda Depot for training. Sonny and his mother knew dirty black scoudrels of Guards. They had seen some slow sneakey ones too. Sonny had met one nice fellow, but he was sacked out of the Guards.

He told me about the sneakey old fella who stepped out in front of him one night when he was coming down from Delaney's in Ballyhaunis. He had no front light, no reflector, no brakes and no mudguards. He took Sonny by suprise because if Sonny got on his bike no Guard In Ballyhaunis or Kiltimagh would have caught him in a fair run. So he got summonses – a whole sheaf of them. They were left there on the window. At this point Sonny lowered his voice and he began.

"If I had my wits about me and if I got a really good solicitor he could have proved that I did not have a bicycle at all!"

When he had hammered all the studs into the soles of my new boots I asked how much he would charge me. Nothing! He was giving me this much for good luck.

He suggested with mock outrage that when I became a Guard and met any cyclist that I was to be sure to summons that cyclist for everything that I could think of, like no brakes, no bell, no lights… even if it was in the middle of the day! But if I met a fellow driving an old car and even if he had no tax or insurance or any of them extras, I should shake his hand and say,"Well done my son. You have done well to have as much as you have".

His mother got up from her seat and she pressed a silver coin into my hand. Despite all of his talk to the contrary Sonny knew every Guard for miles around and he was on good terms with all of them.

As I pedalled along past Tarpey's I looked up Peter Duffy's road half expecting to see the old schoolmaster sailing along slowly on his bicycle, but now it is I who am sailing along slowly. I left my bicycle proped against the sod fence and I took a seat on the cool green grass that grew along the fence. I looked along the peaceful narrow road which the master had traversed for forty years. In line with the modern practice of writing a letter which I might have written to Mr Michael John Flanery, I composed the following:

"Dear Mr Flanery.

I am now twenty years older than you were when I used to know you. At the time I considered that you were very old. Since I never had an opportunity to speak to you man-to-man, I now avail of this opportunity. You played a significant part in my formative years. If I remember correctly you were sparing enough in the advice that you gave me, but you knew that it was how you acted, that had most influence on youngsters.

I greatly admired your masterful knowledge of your subjects. The message that you conveyed to me was that it was important to carry out one's duties to the letter of the law. I remember that you were always courteous to all those who visited us from time to time. You never tried to project yourself or seek fame in any way.

At least that was how I saw you, and I greatly admired these qualities. In later life I tried to emulate your methods in my own sphere of life. Looking back over the years I often think that if I had shown more deference to those who could influence my progress I might have been more successful. Nevertheless I am glad that I resisted the temptation to bend my knee to none, but the one true God.

Your words to me when I had moved into fifth class are still fresh in my mind. You remember that you told me that I had neglected my tasks, and that now I could never catch up. In a way you were half-right, but you should have known that I had other obligations to my people at home. Around that time I was becoming useful as a second man on the land. My father also had some fixed ideas, and one of these was that a boy spending too much time at books would be of little use on the land.

The only income that our family had was the meagre income off the land. My family had fallen behind most of the neighbours in the matter of housing. Since I was the eldest son it behoved me to work and help them come abrest of the neighbours. When you told me that I could never catch up I stopped trying. I had no reason to doubt your wisdom. I was lucky enough to meet another great teacher, and he told me that it was not necessary to go to school to become educated. All that you have to do, he said, is to read good books intelligently, and I have been trying to do this ever since.

The conventional wisdom was and still is that education obtained from a proper school is the only real education. I believe that you knew better. In your wide reading you must have come across some of the great masters of the English language who used to sit outside the church at night, and read passages with the aid of the outside light of the church – their families being so poor that they had no light in their dwellings.

A few weeks ago an eminent professor wrote on how he lectures to students who would benefit more if they read the text books at home. So you see, eductation in a formal institution is not always what it seems. Think of all the youngsters who left off primary school feeling that they could never catch up.

You had books in plenty in the press, at school. I often stood to look at them, but you never offered one of them to me to read. Nor did you ever even give me the name of a good book that I might read. A few years later I had an opportunity to visit regularly, Webbs second-hand book shop, on the quays in Dublin. The first book that I ever bought there was the Vicar of Wakefield. We had an extract from this book in our sixth class English reader. I read this book at least twice, and I still have that copy.

I do not blame you for telling me that I could never catch-up. You had been living in your own cuckoo-land, and it was less trouble to you, to dismiss your past-pupils, and let them go off into another world beyond Hollyhead. However it may have been that you really believed that your past-pupils had a more fulfilled life than you had yourself. I must compliment you in some respects; you never spared yourself in your efforts. I must also add that many of your students could have sat for the Parish Priest's examination[1] after the completion of sixth class.

Yours faithfully,

Joe Coen.

Leech's old house is gone. I remembered Jim Grady who was a

---

[1] *Parish Priest's examination was an examination which curates of mature years had to pass before being considered for selection for Parish Priest.*

steward there and a decent man he was when he distributed the fruits of the orchard. This had been the home of a landlord named McDonell.

I remember driving cattle to the fair in Kiltimagh and you could be sure that Leech's gate would be closed. The next little road up by Eddie Boyle's was a place where I had a few hard runs chasing cows, but once we got to the Cahir Cross, the animals seemed to give up trying to go back home.

The same Cross was the scene of great Land League activity. Michael Davitt had picked up a few tricks from the Trade Unions in England and he often outwitted the authorities. One day, a widow woman was to be evicted, so people from miles around brought material to build a new house for her. The house was built in one day, half on her own land and half on her neighbour's land. When she was ordered out of her new house, she simply went across to the room that was now in her neighbour's land, and so the warrant for her removal did not apply. Then, after the Sherrif and his agents left, she was back, again. With the help of the people Davitt so frustrated the Landlords that they were glad to sell out and go away. Very little is now known in his native county of the man who devoted his life to helping the small farmers.

The land on each side of the road on the way into Kiltimagh is of poor quality. Despite this many good animls were driven down the little roads on each side along the way. The people too seemed to me to be good looking, at least the girls were; I did not look at the men very much. I could still name a dozen of the finest-looking girls you could ever see. I hope that the years have been good to them, for they deserve to be rewarded for their kindness. Their smiles and good humoured banter did so much to cheer the weary and impovrished travellers from the east.

The middle men or 'sharks' who bought animals to sell again later, at the very same fair, used to come out the road to meet us. These people hoped they might meet some uninformed person who'd sell his animals cheap. To be fair to these sharks, they added a bit of excitment and alerted the weary cattle drovers who had been up since

29

three or four o'clock in the morning, and who had been sprinting and doing some long-distance runs as well. In those days, some of the animals cut a strange figure. Many of them had very big heads and big, long horns, which showed that they were old, but had experienced starvation. Some of the animals too had big bellies and short legs. Not suprising that the owners became annoyed if their animals became the subject of comicial comments.

"Are you selling the Handlebars?" one would shout with reference to an animal with a long pair of horns.

"How much for the ould henhouse?" another would shout with reference to the bird droppings on the animal's back.

"Are you selling the schuttery calfeen?"Which latter comment was not very complimentary to the owner walking behind his "bullock".

Such colourful comments livened up the atmosphere, but we made no effort to do business until we had our beasts standing on the footpath looking into Mick Patsy's Bar. Like so many of our old haunts M. P. Walshe's is also closed. For old time's sake I had intended to treat myself to one glass of red lemonade, and a few fig rolls.

4

Dubh Garradí or Black Garden

THE NEAREST HOUSE to ours was about three hundred yards out the little road and across what is now the N17. It was in a different townland to our house, but I was almost as familar with this house as I was to our own house. In the old days it was a lively place. There was always much signs of life about it. Pigs seemed to be always squealing, and hens cackling, and calves lowing and people shouting. The people who lived in that house were big with loud voices. Sometimes they sang, and sometimes they played musical instruments. They often shouted at one another. Mick—the man of the house—the daddy of them all, was a big man with a rugged face and a big white moustashe. You could hear his big strong voice for miles across the countryside.

Another of our neighbours took pride in being different to the rest. On a good summer day, when everyone else was taking advantage of a fine day to settle up the hay, he would just tie his coat on the carrier of his bicycle and set off cycling to one of the cities, which invariably was either Galway or Sligo. The cyclist would have barely cleared out of view when the big voice would ring out; "Its all very fine for some people!"

Mick's house was big and generous like the people who lived there. It had been a long, low house with four windows to the front. Mick raised it to a two-storey and slated the roof over three windows. He left one room of the house low, and covered that part of the roof with galvanise. He did nearly all of the work himself for as they say, he had a great pair of hands. He once told me how he plastered his house. He dug up gravel in the hill-field and he sifted the round pebbles out of the gravel and he put these into sacks. Now, he would rub on some plaster on an area of the walls and while the plaster was still soft, he would take fistfulls of the pebbles and throw them at the soft plaster. He was endowed with the biggest hands that I have ever seen. The plaster with the pebbles is as well fixed now a hundred years later as it was the year that he had the job finished

The windows seem to have become smaller than I remember them. Perhaps it is the virginia creeper which has grown wild, especially around the windows. Otherwise the house is as solid as ever. The slates are level and are holding on well. As I stood there remembering, I suddenly became sad and lonely. The silence was uncanny. The mid-day sun threw an almost accusing look so that I hurried away lest I should intrude anymore.

The next house is also vacant and so I hurried past. I just threw a quick look up at the bungalow on the hill, for music, loud talk and wittisims came easily from there too. I imagined that I heard the sound of a football rolling through the clouds of time.

The blacksmith's house, though vacant, is newly painted. It fits in with the replacement forge which the roadmakers have substituted for the real forge which they rolled into the new road. I stood in on the narrow grass verge to wait for the memories of old to come floating back into my mind. I could see again the wide open door of the old forge. The sparks came flying from the workings and and I could hear the slow measured beat on the anvil. I often watched the blacksmith as he hit one blow on the red iron and then let the hammer hop two or three times before he'd strike the iron again. Once, when I was very young, I used to think that he was as interested in the music of the anvil as he was inhammering the stubborn iron. I could stand for hours just watching this man at his work. On other days he would be shoeing wheels.

In those days, the wheels of horse-drawn vehicles were made of wood with an iron rim on the outside which was called a tyre. The wooden wheels were made with a centre called the stock and spokes were carefully morticed into the stock and then every two spokes were driven into a section of the circle which was called a felloe. These were painted in a bright orange colour and they were left outside the forge door. The blacksmith prepared the tyres for these wheels

The tyres were left on a stone platform and a layer of turf was built around them and then the turf was ignited and so the ring of fire was watched until, in the opinion of the blacksmith, the tyres had reached the optimum temperature. The blacksmith and a helper armed with a long handled crook in each hand lifted each tyre and placed it over the new wheel. The wheel had been placed on another stone platform with a hole in the centre to allow the stock to go into the hole and so that the wheel sat steadily. When the tyre was in situation the two men ran with buckets of water to cool the tyres so that the iron rim rapidly contracted and became tight, and held the whole wheel firm.

I remember the blacksmith for his sense of humour. In some respects he remained a boy all of his life. I recall one incident when a very sedate old farmer walked over two miles to visit the blacksmith for some special job he needed to have done at the forge.

"Did you hear that Mick…. gave up smoking?

"I never knew that he smoked. "

"He won't start now anyway. "

"Why?"

"He died last night. "

The old man began to recall all the feats of strength that the deceased had achieved.

"He hadn't all of his toes on one foot. "

Tom Costello
Local Blacksmith

"If you were trying to catch him on the football field or keep up with him on the hayfield, you'd soon discover there was nothing wrong with his feet!"

"I did't say that there was anything wrong with his feet. I just said that he hadn't all of his toes on *one* foot – he had five toes on *each* foot."

"Ah, be damned to this for a lark!" said the old man, and he stormed off and forgot what it was that he came to the forge for in the first place.

33

When motor cars became plentiful, old cars would be left about. Soon it was discovered that the wheels and axles of discarded cars were suitable for the animal-drawn vehicles, and so the era of the blacksmith was over. Some of the blacksmiths began using the electric welders and made gates and other farm implements, but such items made in factories could be produced much cheaper, and so the forges have mostly closed

Just across the high stone wall from the forge stood the local National School. Within these high walls boys and girls were confined for six hours, five days a week. In latter years these young people were required by law to attend these schools until they reached fourteen years of age. Some of the pupils attending these schools learned reading and writing in English and Irish and they became familar with arithmetic. But for a variety of reasons many of these pupils could neither read or write in any language at the end of their term at school. All of them could recite some prayers however, and they were told—and they would forever remember—that there was a God above who would reward the good and punish the wicked.

This old school next to the forge is the "new" school for it replaced an older establisahment that was used as a cow byre until it was rolled under the new road. The first school was established some time after the great famine of 1847, and some of the educated natives objected to these schools as they were afraid that the Irish language would be lost, as it was not taught under the British. Later, under our native government Irish was included, but the people had lost interest in their native language. They felt that their families needed English to get on in the English-speaking world, and so the Irish language is weakening all the time.

Sadly now, I moved on down the road to the next junction with a sign marked "Lurgan". This is what we used to know as the Doogarry road. The land close up to the edge of the road is low-lying and rushes grow fairly profusely. This gives a wrong impression of the land in Doogarry, for there is some good deep soil in the land just away from the edge of the road. The Doogarry farmers used to cut a bit of a dash with their heavy-legged horses trotting with the side-car over the road, to Mass of a Sunday. Lesser farmers would have a horse that was two or three hands lower than those from Doogarry. Some of the Doogarry cattle would shake the road as the farmers chased them into the fair in Kiltimagh.

There used to be at least fourteen homesteads in this townland and now there are only three families still residing on their properties. The remaining farms are farmed intermittently by people who visit once or twice a week. I could count at least twenty young men who left before they were twenty years of age, and there was as many girls if not more. Such a loss to our country and such a gain for other countries, and I do not believe that these countries fully appreciate the wealth that they have been getting over the years.

There is one new house and it is occupied, but not by the family I used to know. Then there is the Eanach, where some used to cut turf of a poor quality. I mentioned the Eanach to a few local young people but this old Irish name for 'the very wet bog' seems to have dropped out of the local vocabulary. I stood on the edge of the road with my back to the Eanach and I looked eastwards up towards the bare hills. The way the sun shone down on the hill, I could see the traces of the ridges which had been made by evicted tenants. Local lore tells that there was a choice of either these bare hills or the wet bog, which could be had at a rate of just one pound per acre.

All of the good land had been fenced off into a farm of one hundred and twenty acres. The landlord, one Mr McDonnell from Cahir (Leetches' old place) rented this farm to a man named Taylor who was a Protestant from Roscommon. In order to produce a crop from such sterile land as was left outside the fence, the trick was to cut off scraws and dry them like turf and then burn them. I found ashes under the sod when a piece of wet bog was ploughed a few years ago. To put a stop to this method of crop production, a special act of Parliment was passed in the House of Commons.

In the end, the deprived tenants assembled one morning on the top of these hills and they stood looking back at the townland of Clooncah, where their homes had been for many generations. Some of the women and children in the group started up a loud crying and wailing as was often practised at funerals. A local woman who was

35

a child at the time often spoke of how sad and lonely this cry was. Finally, the whole group set off walking to catch the train in Ballaghaderreen. From there they got a train to Dublin, and then on a boat to Liverpool. That generation of the people were always out of their homes in England, waiting to meet their old neighbours from Bruff and local townlands.

Bearna Esker is still used as a place name. Cloon Tuirc is now known as Woodfield. In the old days the English could not get their tongues around some of our place names, indeed they did not try too hard, so they gave places names that came more easily to the English tongue. The modern Irish have now become much the same as our former masters.

The mention of Esker reminds me of one particular indivudal who has not been rewarded or recognised for his enterprising work on behalf of the community. When some warriors returned back from England with their pockets full, they used to go to Kilkelly and enjoy a few drinks. Feeling in high good humour, they used to feel like engaging the whole community in their reverly. They would go into farm yards and release the pigs, and the cows, and perhaps take the two wheels off the cart. These pranks caused a good deal of annoyance to the people concerned.

This unnamed individual would lurk unseen, near the edge of the road, amongst some post-glacial ridges of stone and gravel, and he used to cannonade these pranksters with stones. These stones came dropping out of the air not very slowly, and if they dropped on a man's skull they often had the effect of swiftly changing his mood. A few direct hits often encouraged the warriors to retreat home to their mammies. The marksman from the ridgetop was never properly identified, but was simply known as 'Seaneen na gcloc'.

I crossed the road and I read the inscriptions on the commorative monument at the junction of the Kiltimagh road. This is a fitting reminder of the efforts of the men in the fight for our independence. Amongst the names is a kinsman of my own called Michael Coen from near Ballyhaunis, who was shot dead at his farm before the British Forces followed up by slicing his body into pieces with their bayonets. There was no trial, just the word of a distressed woman who had mentioned his name as being involved in an attack on one of the members of the auxillary Police force. I said a prayer for all who lost their lives in the struggle, whoever they were.

Memorial to those who died in defence of the Republic

5

The Baíle (or) The Buaíle

I WAS NOW COMING within sight of the town of Kilkelly, and I decided to swing to my right and head into Cloughwalley. It is summertime and therefore the right time to visit the Buaile. I have never heard of any winter-time visits to the Buaile. The name of the townland gives some history. Clock Buaile; "The Stone Summer Resort." The Buaile was an area of rough grazing used in the summer time by local farmers. Over time these rough grazing areas were taken over by settlers who built houses there and fenced in the grazing area and treated them as their own land.

Our ancestory had some uppish notions of going to the lakeside for the summer. Instead of making up fences on the farm, the womenfolk used to take the livestock with them to Cloughwalley and leave the men to get on with the tillage work. The only residue of this notion was one of 'minding the cows'. This notion of minding the cows applied where animals were let loose where tillage areas were not fenced in.

I remember many years ago when I visited a relative in the adjoining parish and it was a wet day. A man from the house next door was visiting, and from time to time he used to get up and open the back door to look at his cows to ensure that they did not go into the field of oats. This was the only incident of 'cow minding' that I have ever witnessed. I have however, heard of another reference to this traditonal chore of 'minding the cows'. Apparently when P.D. Kenny, the distinguished writer was a boy at home in Lismegansion, he used to be engaged in 'minding the cows' for his parents. Sometimes he would bring the spade along – not to make up a fence apparently – but to cut out angles and squares and so familarise himself with trigonometry. There are also references to herding in Donegal in

Seamus Mac Manus' "Lad of the O'Friels". So it seems they did not make fences much in Donegal either.

Even as far back as when P.D. Kenny was a boy - twenty years after the famine, Clock Buaile was out of bounds. One could speculate that a few of the seasonal visitors became so fond of Cloughwalley that they opted to remain there all the time. I remember a few very self-confident farmers who might not be too pleased to have their rich farmland's name translated and interpreted as above.

There was a lot of wisdom in the notion of clearing out the animals from the farm buildings for a few months of the summer. I remember one summer the hens in my mother's flock began to drop off one by one. It was a serious matter, because the hens provided the petty cash for our household, and indeed for most farmers at the time.

Experts were consulted on the way home from Mass, but no remedy was suggested except to get rid of hens altogether out of the place, for a year or two. This was not a very satisfactory solution. To put an end to all of the speculation, my father got a few large sacks and he packed the hens into these bags one night and he brought them up to the end of the lane where there was an old lime-kiln. He dumped the hens into the limekiln and he laid a few branches of thorn bushes across the mouth of the kiln, and he covered this over with rotted hay from the butts of hay cocks.

Old limekiln

At least the hens were out of sight, and my mother was inclined to forget about them. After a few days one or two hens escaped and then the whole flock began to fend for themselves eating snails and frogs and anything that they could find. After about a month the hens got a bit red about the gills, and you could hear them going about the fields "singing". They returned to sleep in their new house in the lime kiln and before long they began to lay eggs in little nests that they formed from some of the rotted hay.

Their old hen house was now swept out and the floor and perches doused with fistfulls of lime. There was great jubliation in our house when the hens were restored to their old home. Each year after that our hens were given a summer holiday in the lime-kiln.

I remember the first time that I heard the place of Cloughwally translated and explained to me. I had an image of local women driving off the cows down the road towards Kilkelly and then stopping and allowing them to graze along the side of the hills. I had figured that these women would have tin saucepans tied together and swung over their shoulders rather like the travelling folks.

The grown-ups had completely abandoned the notion of a sojourn to Cloughwally for the summer, but in our time as youngsters we did our best to revive the practise. Once the snow had gone from the valleys we were getting ready to go fishing to the lakes in Cloughwally. Each year the fishing rod had to be replinished. The new perch line and a few hooks were provided in Kilkelly by Leo Duffy. The fishing rod was a home-made affair. A long straight handle a bit longer than the brush handle was ideal. If you were lucky enough to have a handle off a wooden rake it was ideal and then all that was required was a piece of tubular iron. About twelve inches off the cross bar of an old bicycle was ideal. You hammered the tubular partially up the rake handle and then you procured a third year growth of a willow. These grew in every garden in those times.

The float was also provided by Mr Duffy, who also ran a pub, and so the cork off a stout bottle provided this element of the fishing gear. The cork floated on the top of the water and when this began to dip excitement began. A hooked fish pulled the cork down out of sight.

Experience told you how to regulate the cork. On bright days it was found that fish remained in deep waters, but on a dull day the fish came closer to the surface, and you adjusted your cork accordingly.

The bait used was often gauged by the weather and the time of the year. The good red worm found on the edge of the farmyard manure pit was the usual bait. In early summer the 'leather jacket' which is the larvae of the 'daddy long legs' could sometimes be very effective.

In an age when older people are often shoved into homes for the bewildered, careful reflection should be given to the ways that our ancestors lived. There is much to be learnt from Cloughwalley of the olden times, but Cloughwalley also has some modern industry too. The post-glacial sands are now being used to make concrete blocks to build towns and cities far away. The gravel and the water is there in plenty, and it is good to see that local men and women can now be employed outside their own doorstep, instead of being a spailpin in some other country.

Sadly there is so much more to be done. The fertile fields with the warm limestone underneath could grow again the floury potatoes and the sweet vegetables that once grew in every garden. The skills that were so essential then, are now in danger of being lost. Beef production is being promoted, which is fine for those who have a few hundred acres of land. We seem to take our copy from either the USA or Australia where a farm of a few thousand acres is normal. When will someone just mention the fact that we have a finite acreage of land in Ireland? The fact is that more food could be produced off one acre of land than by growing grass for feed for cattle or sheep and then killing them for meat. We could show the world how it is done, if only we had the same quality of agricultural leadership as is shown in the gravel industry.

6

Lísmegan and Ballína Costello

A COOL AND GENTLE breeze was coming from the Kiltimagh direction and it nudged me to turn left towards Aghamore. The many happy days and nights that I spent around the Bruff Crossroads are now as fresh on my mind as if those days were as recent as last week. Many who look back on those years long ago when we were growing up might say that we were deprived, and underprivleged. If so, we certainly were not short of public parks wherein we could play. Practically every field was available to us, but we did not chose to use many of these. We did however frequently use Newell's sraith, because of its proximity to the Bruff Crossroads where the youth used to meet. The sraith was so called because it was a bit waterlogged on or near the boundry.

The first circus that I ever saw was in Newell's sraith. I was about four years of age, and it was the only time that I can remember when our entire household went out together. We set off together across the fields to the circus. Up in our hill-field my father lifted me up in his arms so that I could see the big tent. I remember that it was blue in colour – or so it appeared to me - and it reminded me of the Cloughwalley lake which I had seen once. I remember very little of the circus except that the clown looked a bit like my father when he was ready to begin shaving.

Later on I often took a part in football practce games that we used to have in Newell's sraith. Mr Newell and his neighbour James Casey owned the farm in a sort of joint ownership and it was operated on the rundale system. This was a system where the land rotated each year from one farmer to the next. In actual event, neither farmer had any great interest in manuring the land because it was the neighbour of course, who would benefit by use of it the following year. In these neglected circumstances the land became greatly run down. In my memory the farm was not used at all by Casey, and Newells only had a donkey or sometimes two donkeys. Not surprisingly, the Newell-Casey farm was the last place in our locality where the rundale system was operated. A little farther on is Patrick Lyons' workshop. The surname "Lyons" is (or was) so numerous in that area that nicknames had to be invented to identify the different families. However Patrick got away with his full real name.

On the northern side of the road here the ground rises rapidly, and on the other side of the road there is a deep valley, and a swallow-hole where the water from the Newell's sraith and other places gushes down whenever there is a downpour. The water that goes down in that hole comes out at Tobar Cainthe in the town land of Tubber about a mile away. Sappers who were working in the area once put the chaff from the oats down into the swallow-hole and some of the chaff came out at Tober Cainthe. If they were able to interpret the cainthe (or chatter) coming from the well they might have heard some interesting news.

Above the swallow-hole there is a steep rise in the land. When I was about six years of age myself and another boy stood at the gateway on the side of the road, looking southwards over the valley and on to the hill beyond. I remember seeing men with hammers up on a galvanised roof. I could see the lift and fall of the hammers but the sounds took longer to reach me so it seemed that their hammering was out of sequence. This was the first time that I had perceived this phenomenon. Ever since that day whenever I hear hammering on galvanised iron I am reminded of that day, and a feeling of melancolic nostalgia comes over me.

All of the buildings on the farm were thatched, except this one which had recently been re-roofed with galvanised iron. The owner of the place had a particularly good year working for farmers in England, and he used the extra money to roof

A typical period farmhouse

the barn. He had planned to re-roof all of his buildings with galvanise, and then re-roof his dwelling house with slates. In the meantime however, his wife had been accused of 'sinning' while her husband was away and she was banished from our parish and sent to a distant part of the country, taking her three children with her.

The local Parish Priest took charge of the whole business and the local people took no part. The people were greatly saddened to see the break-up of a family. The "forgivness of sins" and "the new and eternal covenant" seemed to have another side to it, and this side always seemed to fall heavier on the poor.

The matter was never much discussed amongst the people. Things had not changed, and I believe that the community minded its own business, and just looked the other way. This indifference to the misery of others is something that seems peculiar to rural Ireland. Michael Davitt wrote at some length on this peculiarity of character. He was refering to the people who died during the great famine. He was ashamed of his fellow Irishmen who could just lie down on the side of the road, eating grass, while ignoring the awful screams of their wives and children as they lay dying the dreadful death of hunger. "The animal in the field. . " Davitt said, "would fight rather than die with hunger!" He was right in that because in 1947 – the year of the big snow – a neighbour of ours had no fodder for his animals, and they smashed their way into my father's haggard. He tried to beat them back, but as he said they were gone fhiane with the hunger. They wouldn't just lie down and die. With good rations it is hoped that we have recovered some of the older fighting spirit. Perhaps suffering from hunger for a long period during the famine, does induce an unnatural resignation to 'the will of God'.

Almost directly across the road from this gateway was the residence of a retired blacksmith named Tom Newell. He did not look much like the village Blacksmith as depicted in Longfellow's Poem. His arms did not seem to be as strong as iron bands, more like the legs of a skylark. However what he may have lacked in brawn he made up for in wit. He always claimed that he had the strength of his profession, and so a boy of about fourteen was matched against him in a wrestling match. With one wrench the boy had the smith on the ground and they rolled under the table where the light of the oil lamp did not reach.

"Now! Have you had enough of it?" Shouted the smith.

A sensible man peered under the table and he saw that the boy had his man down and was sitting on top of him. To save face in the presence of the smith's wife, Mrs Newell, the man appealed to the smith to please release the boy and so the smith came out from under the table in apparent triumph. The only trace that a dwelling stood on the hill where Newells once lived is a few evergreen shrubs. There is absolutely no trace of Casey's anymore.

Having lingered along the Aghamore road I now spin up the road to Ballina Costello. This is the old road to Knock. The road going up by Cruach abhaine is a new road. I remember some old people in Curhavnagh refering to this road as "the New Line". The Curhavnagh road was made as part of the relief work during the great famine of 1847, and it is probable that the road through the bog was also made at this time. My mother's grandfather Mick Boyle worked on this famine relief work on the Curhavnagh road. His salary was a stocking of oatmeal per day. Plastic bags were not available in those days and if paper bags were used they would tear with the wet.

The road going through Ballina Costello may be an old road, but there are a great many new luxurious dwellings on it today. The older houses – which were the only ones that I could identify – are also painted in bright colours which add a sense of cheerfulnees. I think that Michael Turpin's house must be knocked down. The next house, Willie Yank's, is newly painted. These are, or were, both Lyons'. I could see that Willie Lohan's house is occupied. Paddy Coleman's house is in a very fine state of repair and so is Sonny Lyons'. I stood looking at yet another residence formerly occupied by Martin Lyons and his son Tommie.

I remembered Tommie (who was a bit of a trickster) telling us about the visiting chimney sweep who came to do his thing on Lyons' chimney. Tommie lived in a one-storey house while Maggie Byrnes owned a two-storey house close beside. The chimney-doctor added about five of his sticks to the brush that he was poking up the chimney, and asked Tommie to go out and have a look to see if the brushes were protruding out of the chimney pot.

"No sign of it" said Tommie.

The man added a few more rods and invited Tommie to have another look.

"Still no sign".

Finally the bewildered man added all of the extension rods that he had, and then he went out himself and had a look. By this time the brush-head was towering well over Maggie Byrnes' house. Good cheer was always in plentiful supply in that area.

I stood looking down south towards the river valley. The sun was shining now on where the old fairgreen had recently been mowed. The scene to me reflected the good cheer that had been a part of the old Ballina Costello. Great fairs used to be held here. Animals were offered for sale and this activity enticed all sorts of traders. There is an old dresser in our house that my great-grandmother Biddy Mc Nichols bought at the fair in Ballina Costello. It was made by a man named Egan from Cloonterrif, which is only a few miles up the road.

The venders of illicit spirits used to frequent the place too, and so did the knitters of socks. These socks came in different sizes. Some were used to measure oatmeal and other socks were used for 'military purposes' so to speak. The idea was to get a round stone of about a pound weight and drop it into the sock. You took a hold on the top of the sock and swung it at shoulder height. In this manner a small man could even-up any size-difference with a bigger man. Indeed it was not unknow for some of the lady vendors of wares to use this weapon as a means of asserting their authority.

For months before the fair, young men would have suitable blackthorn shillelaghs seasoning up their chimneys, in preparation for the fights that took place in Ballina after the main business of the day was done. The men from Aghamore used to line up against warriors from the Knock parish and they got in close

combat until one team or the other was depleted through knock-outs. My mother used to tell of the dent that her grandfather, Mick Boyle had on his skull as a result of a blow from an Aghamore man at one of these meetings at Ballina.

A gentle breeze came up from the river just cooling the hot summer day. I remembered the story of a man who got work cleaning the river one winter. At about half past seven in the morning, when it was still dark, the man was facing out to go to his job. A shower of sleet was blowing from the southeast, and when the man got clear of the shelter of his own house he got a full blast of it. He turned back home and proceeded to unfasten the tethers that kept the cows tied at the end of the kitchen. The cows were not suprisingly slow to leave the shelter and the noise woke up his wife who was snugly sleeping in the hag.

"O the lord save us! Why are you putting out the cows of a morning like this?"

"If it is too cold for the cows, 'tis too cold for me. "

So he joined his wife in bed in the hag, and gave the river-cleaning a miss for that day.

The proximity of the river was a great source of recreation especially for those boys and men who took an interest in fishing. The type of fishing that used to be done along this river was very highly skilled and none but those who were to the river born, so to speak, could master the art. You procured a long rod six or seven feet long and you added a smooth handle onto this. The handle of a hay rake was ideal. You made a snare of a single strand of copper wire and tied this on to the top of the rod. Now you could dangle this snare up river from the fish. The trick was to let the snare down into the water on a level with the fish. With great expertise you got the snare behind the fish's gills and then you lifted the fish clear out of the water. The fish were wiley creatures and if you touched them with the snare before it was in position the fish bounded off. The real expert fishermen rarely missed.

Fishing for salmon was illegal in the manner in which it was carried on along the bank of the rivers in our area. The problem was, that when the English took over our country (because they had a much bigger army) they granted ownership of the land to their friends, and the lakes and rivers went with those lands. Now, some of these English people sold on the fishing rights to Insurance companies, and to similar others who had money to spare. You were then supposed to pay these people for the right to fish. But we never really accepted this, and maintained that we had as much right to fish or indeed *more* rights even, than these people. So, it was seen as a kind of 'patriotic duty' for us to fish illegally on our lakes and rivers.

You did your fishing for salmon at night, and you used what was refered to as a 'candle'. This comprised a stick of about five feet long. You dried a dewt sack on the hob for a few hours, and then you wound the sack around the stick tightly, leaving a good piece clear for holding. When you reached the point where you hoped to fish you poured at least a pint of parrifin oil on to the dried sack and then you lit the candle. One man could hold the candle over the water and so spot the fish. Your companion had a weapon with a handle of fourteen feet long on top of which was fixed a worn, four-pronged fork. In some case the blacksmith had fashioned catches on the tops of the prongs somewhat like the barbs on a fishing hook. This weapon was known as a 'spear' and the operator had just one chance to harpoon the fish as it sat in the water. An experienced fisherman seldom missed.

I lived over a mile from the river and so I seldom had an opportunity of perfecting these skills and therefore had little success. I did however, have an opportunity of immersing myself in the waters of the river at least once a year, when we drove our sheep and some neighbours' sheep as well up to the bridge at Ballina, where the older men would urge the sheep right up to the edge of the river. But the sheep needed more encouragement. So, togged out in footballing attire (aka 'swimwear') and standing chest-deep in the current, I would pull each sheep head-first into the water. I would push them around a few times and that was their annual wash. For fairly stupid animals, they used to know how to get out of the river alright, and would then trot off home without once looking back.

7

Aghamore

I BEGAN MY TRAVELS today in Aghamore, where many of my bicycle journeys as a youth had begun. First, I visited St Joesph's Church where, along with two other siblings I was baptised. One was named "Cormac Joseph", another "John Joseph" and yours truly was christened "Thomas Joseph". One of us has already been called to his eternal reward, and I can say for myself that I am in no great hurry to join him. We got a good start in Aghamore and all of us kept the faith.

Still on high ground, I cycled down the road at Bothar na Sop to the place where St Patrick had his first conversions in Aghamore. The saint was attracted there because it was a centre of communal activity long before his time. One can still see ancient monuments including an ogham stone and an old church where people have been buried since at least the fifth century. An old belief remains; that the old church in the graveyard in Aghamore was once sited at Carroneedan, but God Himself caused it to walk down across the fields to where it is now. I have no doubt that God *could* cause the church to walk as described, but surely, God does not show-off in that way, so maybe there's some other explanation?

To the rear of the church I found a headstone to my father's maternal grandfather Sean "Mhaire" Neafsey, and further down is his daughter Bid (my grandmother) and my grandfather Michael Coen. Down in the new graveyard I said a prayer over the remains of

St Joseph's Church, Aghamore

49

my parents, Willie and Nora Coen. I could have spent the whole day reading off the headstones of people that I knew. I saw the names of old men who used to kneel with great reverence with their rosary beads dangling across the back of church pews. If you were looking about you or not behaving as you should, you'd get a jab from one of the big crubs of hands with the encouragment to, "Say your prayers now, good ladeen". No further urging to piety was ever necessary.

I also saw names of people who were young with me, and as I was leaving it occured to me that I was moving up in the line too. I searched around to see if I could find the place where they buried our schoolmaster, the late John James Flanagan, who taught school in Doogarry for nearly fifty years, but I could not find it. Before I left I said an Our Father for his soul and I was very careful say every tittle of it, for that was his way. Whatever you do, do it properly.

I stood for a while looking across the wall down into the valley, and then my eye followed the rising ground right up to the airport. The stone walls climbing northwards almost as far as the eye could see. These walls running parallel and fairly close giving an impression of long, narrow fields, rather like the fields uncovered at the Ceide Fields at the northern end of the county.

The Raith Castle seemed to break into my view wherever I looked. Those old Normans who came to our shores many thousands of years ago liked to be conspicious. The memory of their presence is still

Raith Castle

impressed upon us. Other visitors had come before them – also uninvited – and they too left their mark, but in more subtle ways. Their handiwork could be explored under the green sod, but it lies there mostly unknown. I remember many years ago after a wet spell in the summer an unexpected breach in the ground ocurred, and a cave underneath the sod became visible. This 'cave' was high enough for a man to stand upright. A few of us young boys cycled down after Mass on a Sunday to have a closer look. But the mysterious hole had already been closed up to make the grazing safe for stock.

Some day a great wind will come and knock the old castle down. Perhaps we will then find some other, even more ancient ruins under that old castle.

People came to our Island. Some remained and became part of our race. Now we have new people coming from Europe and soon they will become as Irish as any of us. Our time is transient, and soon, like all of those around me in this place – I too will get the call. If they all arose up about me just now, I'd say that there would be quite some crowd in Aghamore.

Now that I look back it seems to me that Aghamore was always crowded with people. I would be sent off twice a week with ass-and-cart to collect merchandise for man and beast, and there were always a few others waiting to get loaded at the stores – or offering their services. Two shops in Aghamore provided for all kinds of goods. There were three places where you could become drunk, and you could also take home a barrel of nine, or of eighteen gallons. I often heard the old people telling how it was customary to have a nine-gallon barrel for after the hay or the harvest. The bigger barrel was used when you had to bury a man as he lived - decent.

You could get just about everything that a household needed in Aghamore. You could buy a new hayshed, and the timber and slates and cement for a new dwelling house. You could also book your passage to America, or buy a long suit to wear when you died, and there was even a motorised hearse to convey you feet-first down Bothar na Sop to the final resting place. To be ready for such an eventuality there were two Masses on all Sundays and on 'holidays of obligation'. The situation was that whenever I visited Aghamore as a youth it was crowded with people. Now, whenever I go through Aghamore, it almost always deserted.

In the old days Aghamore was a sort of a metroplis. A man

intendening to visit the place would rub the yard brush on his boots and always put on a good jacket. People from close to Ballyhaunis used to do their shopping here and right up to the bridge of Kilkelly people would come to Aghamore to get their needs.

The citizens of Aghamore felt a bit privleged. You'd see them going in to Mass of a Sunday dressed in the latest fashions and usually, they carried a big prayer-book with a clasp. They paraded right up to the front of the church. The proletariate on the other hand waited humbly outside until the last bell had rung, before taking a last few quick pulls out of the woodbine and then sneaking in quietly and standing behind the church door. Some would produce a set of rosary beads and recite a few mumbled 'Hail Marys'.

Not all of the citizens of Aghamore were privileged. I remember one lady of modest means. She lived in a small house with her husband – a gentle and unassuming man. His wife carried herself with some authority; a civil lady, always occupied with the affairs of life. She did, however seem to have a flair for business as good as any of her affulent neighbours. She felt that simply having a shop window on one end of your house and your name over the door did not automatically convey business acumen. On one occasion her husband took a fleece of sheepswool to one of the shops and sold it. Later on, this lady returned to the shop complaining that her timid husband did not get the full price.

"I put the fleece of wool on the scales there, and I gave him the price that was due. "

"Did you now? Well, I am not satisfied that you gave him the full amount, and now I want my fleece back!"

"But how can I pick out your wool out of the hundreds of fleeces in the store?"

"I'd know my own fleece, and I want it back because you did not give us the full price!"

"Well how much do you say the fleece was worth?"

"You only gave him half the price!"

Then the shopkeeper went to the till and he took out the amount which the lady demanded.

"You took advantage of my man because he is a bit soft!

"Mmn. . Well, nobody can say that *you* are a bit soft, Missus!"

———

Wherever you go from Aghamore you will have a good start, for it is five hundred feet above sea level. The sun was now directly over my head and I could see the blue hulk of Neifin Beg, and a bit farther on I could see that blue spire of Cruac Padraig. The hills beyond Kiltimagh looked as if a giant had just thrown a patchwork quilt over a clamp of deserted turf. From a distance even these poor hills looked to be a vibrant green. I came speeding down Finnegan's hill and along by Logbrack until I came to Tobar Na Shraithe.[1] This was a great landmark in the old days. If you were going to Mass and the first bell went off when you were at the well, then you'd be in time. From our house, if the wind was coming from Tobar na Shraithe in the winter, it was understood as a sure sign of snow. There was an old schoolmaster living north-west of us and he used to swear that the winter wind from Tobar na Shraithe always brought snow. In his old age his mind used to wander, and when he was lodging with some relatives in Ballinlough and a cold winter wind was blowing, he would caution the neighbours that the wind from Tobar na Shraithe would soon be bringing them snow. These people had never heard of the famous well, but they believed the old schoolmaster all the same, for indeed, it did in fact snow.

On the oposite side of the road and a little farther on there is a whole range of ancient burial sites. I often heard my father say that when the Aghamore road was being repaired they were digging sand out of a hillock in what was Phillips' and now is part of Kevin Byrne's. The workmen came across a large brown flagstone which they identified as not being indigenous. They suspected that it might be a part of an ancient monument and so they stopped digging and notified the RIC who were in Kilkelly at the time. It appears that Sergeant Parick Lyons was in charge of Ballyhaunis at the time and so he came

---

[1] *The well of the spreading ground.*

down to see what had been found.

Mr Lyons was an eminent antiquarian, who has done more than any other individual to put our part of Mayo on the map in relation to ancient monuments. With a name like Lyons you might expect that he was from Aghamore or Ballyhaunis. In fact Patrick Lyons was born in a place called Lisronagh, in Co Tipperary. His people were evicted off their land, and he was born in a landless cottage. At the age of eleven he got a job from a local farmer, walking about in a cornfield to frighten away the crows. Later he graduated to become a farm worker. There was an RIC station adjacent to the farm and the young Lyons became acquainted with some members of that organisation, and so he became a member.

His first station was in Co Longford, but he spent most of his service in Co Mayo. When he was promoted to the rank of Sergeant he got to know the noted archcaeologist H. T. Knox, who resided near Ballinrobe. This gentleman belonged to the wealthy landed gentry. He had to retire from the British Foreign service in India because of ill health. He began to use Sergeant Lyons to do his outdoor work in relation to archaeology.

Although Lyons came from a most unlikely background to be an archaeologist, he was nevertheless well-qualified. His farming background and his police training eminently qualified him for the job. He also had available to him some strong men who could lift up big stones and save them from destruction. He has the distinction of finding more ogham stones in Ireland, than any other person.

"The Bracklaughboy (Ogham) Stone" near Ballyhaunis

8

Kilkelly

I MOVED INTO THE hard shoulder and then left the N17 and pedalled on to Bridge Street in Kilkelly. The town has expanded, but little since I first visited the place many years ago. This was the first town that I had ever visited, and at the time I felt that it was an imposing metroplis. My mother and my sister not much older than me—but who was years ahead of me—accompanied me that day. My sister was an experienced shopper in the town. They were chatting away the way that women do, and I was just gawking about me. All of the houses seemed to be stuck together, and there were so many shop windows. I saw one man standing outside with a new suit and a hat on him, and I saluted him and bid him the time of day. He made no reply, and I was thinking that these 'townies' were a conceited lot.

My sister was breaking her heart laughing, and my mother too was enjoying some joke of their own.

"Come along now and we will go up the town to Connolly's they often have some toys".

I speeded up a bit and soon we were in this fine shop with all sorts of fancy-coloured boxes. They were talking to my mother, and my sister was getting her speak in now and again. A grey-haired man came over to talk to me. He did not have the handball I wanted but he said he might be getting some in soon, but because of the war everything was scarce. Then he told me of a man he had heard of who kicked a ball so high up in the air that when it came down there was snow on it! I did not know whether to believe him or not, but as I got older, I would often kick the ball high in the air near to those white clouds, and I was just hoping that maybe one time a dusting of snow might return on it.

When we were leaving Conolly's the man went to a jar and he took out a great fistful of sweets and he shared them with me and my sister. As we were coming down the hill I took a look back to see if the man with the hat was still standing there but he had gone inside and he was looking out one of the big windows. As soon as I saw him I shouted in through the shop window but still he took no notice of me. The ladies resumed their laughter again and then my mother put her hand on my shoulder and said;

"Arrah a graeen, sure its not a man – only a model. "

"What's a model?"

"A man made of paper. "They continued to laugh and I figured that they were laughing at me so I sulked a bit and I kept my mouth shut. I still kept looking about for there were so many wonders all about me. We went into a shop where we met the owner Mrs Grennan. She was a teacher, but not a bit like any teacher I had met before. She seemed to be very much like any ordinary woman, she did ask me some questions about figures, she said that I was very good.

After that she took a long glass from inside the counter and she filled it with red lemonade, and she gave me a heap of biscuits on a plate. I took these down to a stool and I left them there and got down on my knees where I could look out the door and take an occasional sip from the lemonade to dampen the biscuits. I remember then a very heavy shower, I was watching the plated rivulets of water coming along by the edge of the footpath. Whenever in later life I see water coming along by a footpath I remember the happy time when I was drinking red lemonade and eating biscuits. Sometimes, for the sake of old times, I buy red leomanade and biscuits, somehow, they don't taste as good any more.

I was reluctant to leave when our business was done that day. Ever since I have felt at home in Kilkelly. In later years I used to visit the town on market day with my father. He used to bring potatoes, turnips and oats for sale. Sometimes he'd only bring turnips filled like you'd fill turf – all loose into the cart. Turnips were cheap, at just two shillings a hundredweight, so he never weighed them. He had a special sack – an old sugar sack – and the fill of this was taken to be a hundred. My father was a regular attender at the market, and he was known to have reliable goods. He usually sold his stuff first and then any new seller would then be asked to sell. One big elderly man arrived with a well-painted cart pulled by a big grey ass. Once he stabled his ass he began to sell. The first customer arrived with a clean new sack, and they began to fill it with turnips. Soon the little donkey's cart was beginning to empty the seller was worried that his whole cart of turnips would fit into the big bag.

"I think that you have a hundred there. " He shouted, but the buyer insisted that it was a sugar bag and so it should be full.

"You surely have a hundred there. "

"No it's a sugar bag. "

"I don't give a danmn if it was a tae bag! You have a hundred there!" Shouted the old man in obvious bad temper.

Some days the buying would be very slow, and father used to say that he'd be bringing his load home again. Then one of the shopkeepers would send his man across the square to get a bag of turnips or of potatoes. Then, in a half an hour the cart would be empty and father would have the one bottle of stout which he allowed himself on such occasions.

When I could ride the master's bicycle I was often sent to Kilkelly on errands for the master to get copies or steel pens. There was anything that any household might need for sale in the town. There were many shops that supplied hardware for use on the farm. There was even a builder's suppliers. Indeed, whatever you needed for the living or for the dead – it could be obtained in Kilkelly.

In the early ninteen-hundreds some of the shopkeepers in small towns enjoyed a very high standard of living. They had maids upstairs and downstairs, and they had shop assistants by the dozen, and finally the lowlies of them all; the yardmen who were generally treated with little respect. These shopkeepers emulated the privleged classes at home and abroad. The staff were taught to treat family members with deference, as they felt was due to them. You didn't call for 'Jim' or 'Mick', but for "Master James" or "Master Michael" and the girls were refered to as "Miss Margaret", and so on. .

These shopkeepers were able to maintain this standard, because of the dense population in the area and all of them charged top penny for their goods. It must be said that nearly all of these shopkeepers gave out credit and they stood a very good chance of getting their money back with interest. The people were devout catholics and were taught that if you did not pay all of your lawful debts you were in danger of loosing your imortal soul. The rates of interest varied and it was rarely specified in clear terms. Often, the interest was a shilling a month in the pound, which would calculate as a most substantial interest – somewhere around 5% today.

Many of the staff members working in these places were the children of parents who owed a bill. The parents felt under such pressure that when the shopkeeper asked to have John or Mary come to work for him, they could not refuse such an offer. In theory the wages coming to these workers was supposed to pay off the bills. But often, the interest charged was in excess of the wages so that instead of the bill becoming smaller, it actually grew. Finally, a few members of the family went off to England, and saved enough money to clear the bills.

From their point of view the shopkeepers felt that they were carrying out the usual business of squeezing as much for themselves as the circumstances would bear. To cover themselves in the hereafter, most shopkeepers had one or two sons in the priesthood and almost invariable they had a daughter or more in the convent as nuns. These family members would, it was felt, regularise things with St Peter.

It must be said that there was a tradition amongst the people that children helped out their parents. They sent money home from England and America to build new houses and often paid for a round-roofed hayshed. The parents used to boast of how well their children were doing abroad. I heard of one man whose older children had already built him a new house and hayshed. Then a younger member crossed over to England and he was earning plenty of money too. The problem for the father was that he could not show this off for he already had a house and a shed, so the only way that he could show everyone how well this younger son was doing, was to speculate on a one-horse mowing machine for the mule.

People living in a modern society in Ireland may find it hard to understand the lack of selfishness of children towards their parents only fifty years ago. At the best of times the ordinary people lived close to the poverty line. The church preached that families should have as many children as possible so that ten or twelve in a family was standard. To feed and clothe such a big household was far beyond that which a migratory labourer could afford. The local shopkeepers did offer credit to prevent starvation however when the children grew up they were expected to help to pay this back with interest.

A family member who did not contribute his or her share would be reminded of their neglect. In the heart of London or way out in West America or in the wilds of Australia someone from home would remind them that they had neglected to do their duty.

Kilkelly c.1960

9

The Road to the Bog

THE ROAD TO the bog is narrow and mostly straight. It runs along the lower end of farmlands and meadowsweet grows in sweet profusion along the edge of most of the roadway. These tall plants with their cream-coloured flowers are inclined to lean towards the centre of the roadway, but so far there is no blockage.

I knew this road very well long ago. I used to stand up on the floor of the ass-cart from where I had a good view of the roadway in front, also of the surrounding countryside. Sometimes, I would urge the ass to a trot but often enough I would allow him to find his own pace which was much slower than a man's standard walking pace. The ass was never in any hurry to reach the bog even though all he had to do there was nibble at the heather bloosoms within the length of the rope with which he was tied. To tell the truth I was in no great hurry to reach the bog myself. But on the homeward voyage the ass seemed to understand my own urgency, he would pick up his tidy little feet and make good tracks home.

Now, as I cycle along slowly I have a fairly good view, the trees have since come into the line of vision. I noted that a few farmhouses are derelict and the eve gutters are swinging in mid-air. I knew some of these farmers who were resident in these houses and even then they were heading for bachelorhood but were still too young to be counted as such. There are also some posh new houses with four-wheel-drive vehicles parked in the yard. These seem to have replaced the ass. There is a look of prosperity around, although I have known some ass owner who were also on very good terms with the Banks.

The road into the bog was the first 'dual carriageway' that I knew. The rules were somewhat similar to those of the M50. You trotted with your beast in on the left hand side, while the horses and carts loaded up with turf came out more sedately on the other side. Nowadays, there is only one track left, here-and-there clumps of black sallies and an occasional furze bush have taken root along the way.

As I walked along this road I searched on the left hand side to see if I could find Tom O'Brien's well, no trace did I find. Indeed the very house where Tom O'Brien used to live is wiped out. This well was a most convenient source of fresh water to workers in the bog. The thirst was not considered urgent enough to allow an adult time to go all the way from the turf face, but a ten year old boy could be spared to be sent on such a mission. Often when 'changing out the turf' I would take a run down as far as the well from the hill. 'Changing out the turf' was a term we used to describe the task of bringing the turf from where it was originally saved to a hill at the beginning of the bog road.

The surface of our bog was so wet and soft that we had to transfer the cut turf onto dry ground where it could be safely loaded onto a horse's cart. Otherwise, the heavy horse and cart would get stuck fast. The smaller ass and cart was used for this purpose. I remember one very wet year when even the ass and cart could not venture into the bog. Some people had to resort to using wheelbarrows to take their turf out, and others carried the turf in a bag on their backs. That was the year when we improvised cleeves and straddles onto the asses back. We made up a straddle with two spikes on which we hung two tea chests. The contents of two tea chests was a good deal more turf than you could load on a wheel barrow or put into a bag to carry on you back. The work was much easier too, but the ass had to do his share.

The heap of turf after the first day's work seemed very small but after a few days it began to grow more quickly. In this way I conveyed the years' supply of turf in the two tea chests.

I stood on the hill looking over the vast area of sedge and heather. The place was quiet and still, completely silent. Not even a bird called. I looked down at Woodfield School. It too stood silent. We used to listen for the cheerful callings of the schoolchildren to tell us the time. After a few minutes silently reminiscing, a few snippets of conversation from long ago came back to me as if it were just happening. I see two men, too young yet to be classed as batchelors. They are walking on each side of an ass and cart. Another ass and his load was hooked onto the the back of the first cart. This was so the two men could converse side-by-side as they slowly made their way zig-zaging out through the bog.

"If I had two more loads out I'd have finished for this year. "

"What the hell do I care. "

Down towards the centre of the bog I can see the blue side-boards of an ass cart, but the ass seemes to have sunk into the bog. The ass's legs are gone down into the soft ground and he seems happy enough to just sit there. The owner-driver is excited and he is shouting for help. One inexperienced worker seems to see some fun in this prediciment but a few of us lift the cart from the ass and then with a little pushing the animal gets up on dry ground.

As I looked about me I could see no sign that anyone has cut turf in this bog for years. Perhaps all of the turf worth cutting has been cut out and so the land will revert to the original owners.

Perhaps it may be that the owners are waiting for the turf to grow again? In the Ceidhe Fields in north Mayo, experts have proved that the layer of turf on the mountainside grew about three metres in five-and-a-half thousand years. It seems to be rather a long time to wait for a fuel supply and even at that, it is not certain that all of the conditions necessary for turf growing are at present available in Freehard.

Perhaps our memories of our experiences in the Freehard bog are not considered worth preserving. One might visulise some sort of a map on the roadside to indicate who had turbary rights in this bog. It might be a nice memory, because many of the descendants of the men who worked the bog are now living in the urban areas of the English-speaking world.

Freehard bog is a relatively small area. I would guess that it is not much over a hundred acres. It is a complete waste as it is. The curlew seems to have fled these shores and the snipe is thin on the ground. There is not food for any other creature except perhaps a few frogs. The area could be put into the production of trees and I believe that trees would grow well and add to the beauty of the area giving a living to many small wild animals.

I remember the first time that I visited the Freehard bog. For me this was purely an excursion for I was barely five years of age. At that time it was a busy place; reeks of turf were all over the hill and out along the road. I remember the brown turf-mould that was blowing in the wind. It was a pleasant experience for me to walk on the soft mould in my bare feet. I remember too that I was anxious to test the waters and despite being warned I ventured into a nice green bunch of grass that grew well in, off the edge. Needless to say the enticing green mound went down under my weight, and so I got my first lesson that green grass in a boghole is not to be trusted.

In a few years I became an old hand myself in the bog, I often enjoyed enticing the innocent "townies" who sometimes came to the bog to walk in on that nice green grass.

10

The Changing Landscape

THE DAY WAS dry and calm—and it was a Sunday—an ideal day, one would think, to go for a cycle down the Boyle Road from Roscommon. But the road is tight and winding and is marked with yellow lines right up to the grass margin. So, the only sensible action for the safety-conscious cyclist is to remain at home. But we cannot all be sensible, so I put the modern equivalent of goose–grease on the bicycle chain, pumped up the tyres, and I ventured forward.

The land on the Boyle side of Roscommon is fertile, and most of the farmers here have five or six times as much as was judged to be 'a viable holding'. I suspect that many of these farmers have been on their land for generations, because in the time of the Landlords their forefathers could make a decent living on land like this, and so could always pay their rent. As a result, they would have stayed on while other poorer neighbours were evicted, and later still, some of those smallholdings would merge into larger farms.

In the olden times, many of these strong farmers used four-wheeled horse-drawn carriages to convey their families on business and pleasure. Early on, they just drove along the fields using the routes used by those on horseback and gradually, roads were built upon these tracks which were naturally winding to suit the horses. Whenever a peasant was met with, he, (the said peasant) was sensible enough to jump out of the pathway of these speeding vehicles.

Modern car-drivers seem to have inherited many of the traits of the old carriage drivers. But the remedy available to the peasants of old is not available to this old peasant today. A portly figure such as myself heading up to four score of years does not have the option of jumping off the road into the field. So I proceed, with extreme caution.

Soon, the beech trees and thorn hedges are replaced by a more open landscape. The fields here are mostly big with stone walls it seems, running along the hills for miles. I stood in off the road to observe more closely. Wondering where did all of these stones come from?

Years ago when landlords swaggered about these fertile lands you can be sure that they did not dig up these stones themselves, so as to leave the land free for the plough and the harrow. The previous occupants of these lands dug up the land to sow their crops. The stones unearthed in the course of this digging were built into walls. As the little holdings were taken over the stone walls were rebuilt to make bigger fields consistent with the bigger farms. Recently, a farmer cultivating his field found a square box made of flat stones about a foot under the surface.

Inside this box was a clay jar. The pottery itself was still intact, but the grain inside had long since disintegrated. The archaeologists told us that the stone box was known as a 'cist' and the grain it had once held was food for someone's journey. This thing was over six thousand years old! They also explained how people had inhabited this particular part of the country then, because it was up above the level of the water that covered the lower areas at the time.

It is reasonable then to infer that people have been living around this area for at least six thousand years. These people came across Europe who believed in cremating their dead. They buried them in an ancient burial chamber. A burial chamber shaped as a box ie; top, bottom and four sides. The chambers were made from flagstone and they usually measured four foot, by two foot, by two foot. These burial chambers are fairly common in County Roscommon. Some of these ancient traditions carried on until Christian Times.

Peoples that came and went since held some different beliefs, some of them believed in cremation for example. Other religions came with the passing of time, and then about two thousand years ago when the waters had lowered a man named Patrick paid a visit. His message was that there was one God who would punish the wicked and reward the good. The law he laid down was that they be good to one another. This belief rested well with their own views, and so they adapted this religion and most local citizens still adhere to this belief system.

The people who settled here would have worked the land intensely, and they lived happily. I have a mental picture of a scene outside one of their modest habitats not so long ago. I can see the man of the house in the light of a harvest moon. He has left a 'scoib'—a flat basket—containing about a stone of floury potatoes on the loose stone wall in front of his house. The wall is gleaming white with a recent coat of whitewash. The man takes a quick glance at the two stacks of oats dominating the settled haystack. His reek of turf is finished down to two sods, and later he plans to dig up sods of sedge grass to roof off his turf for the winter. He carries the scoib of potatoes into the squat whitewashed house and deposits it on the kitchen table, where he is joined by his family for the feast. Each gets a small portion of butter, and a mug of buttermilk. Once the butter supply is exhausted,there is still plenty of salt for the spuds. Some butter would have had to be sold for cash to buy tea and sugar in the local shop.

The farmer may never have been a day in school, but would be possessed of a great store of wisdom passed down from one generation to the next. He knew as if by instinct that his own people had been here since time immemorial – almost certainly for thousands of years. And he is probably right in this assumption. In the course of some excavation work being carried out in County Clare, the body of a young boy was unearthed. It was dated about six thousand years ago. By DNA examination, it was established that three of the children in the local school in 2014 were directly related to this boy. So, there is no good reason to doubt that the man from Roscommon was any more of a traveller, than his neighbour in County Clare.

Over the years, many posh gentlemen had come along holding up pieces of paper signed by Oliver Cromwell or the King of England claiming rights over this little piece of land. But the farmer knew they could not have any legal claim to his land; this land that his own people had worked for thousands of years. The Priest told him that he should pay the rent, but he had no money. All his money had gone in the burying of his father and mother who had recently died.

Before he had time (he got a little warning) to thatch his stacks of oats, a Sheriff accompanied by some local men and about a dozen policemen came to enforce the rent. Their duty was to prevent a breach of the peace, they said. Before these visitors had left that day they had flattened his little house and his barn, and destroyed his stacks of hay and oats. Within a few weeks, he would join six hundred of his neighbours, and they and their families would set sail for Canada.

The Landlord had converted what he termed 'his' estate into farms of over a hundred acres, and in the process had starved, displaced and banished many. Nobody had any right to tell him what he was to do with 'his'land! Before very long he would get his very own personal and permanent share of the land, which was measured 7ft x 3ft, and six-feet-under.

Now a hundred years later pilgrims go to visit the great house where once the Landlord lived. We like to convey to the strangers who come to look at the big house that many of us lived in such houses. The little homes where our ancestors actually lived have long-since been ploughed into the ground, and as far as I know there is not one single original example left standing of the kind of humble place, where our saintly ancestors lived.

Old Irish graveyard

11

Autumn Treasures

LATE INTO OCTOBER and early-November, the autumn landscape shows its most vibrant, delightful colours. For me, the rush of life is over so I can stop and look at scenery at my leisure. The fields are at their loveliest, in their deepest shades of green. Earlier in the year, these same fields were shaved so bare of grass that they looked to be almost white. As if to add insult to injury a big round tank pulled by a dirty green tractor came along and spewed out the filthiest and most foul-smelling liquid, which we in modern times call slurry. The fields seemed at their worst after being splashed with this dark-coloured filth. Then the rains came in an attempt to wash it all away, and the dead bodies of big red earthworms floated in the rivulets of water after each fresh downpour. It was a sad sight, but then, almost imperceptibly, the fields began to recover their natural colour, and now they are at their peak in appearance again.

The trees overhead, their foliage untouched by man, have taken on a whole new range of colours. Shades of lemon-yellow and of lime-green appear, and many shades of red and brown, and indeed even some sprinklings of black. Just about any colour that you could think of is scattered amongst the autumn leaves. If it were possible to list all of the colours, I'm sure we would have to add a few new names as well. It appears that nature is making a last-minute effort to hold on to that precious foliage, giving its fading shelter to the little feathered folk who had frequented the long grass and the trees during the summer.

Many people, even those who are not caught up with the pressures and worries of modern life, just pass these scenes by and never look twice. Others pass by in a blind rush, unaware of the beauty they are missing; the vibrant colours and the subtle changes happening all around them going completely unnoticed. Some others will point to the dramatic splendour of the brown rocky slopes all covered in purple heather that slope into the wild, lapping sea, and talk of the great beauty of nature. I have myself, many times stood on the slopes of the holy mountain, and tried to count the many lonely islands, like lost emeralds set out in Clew Bay.

These scenes are exciting for visitors, but they do not always entertain me, instead they sometimes depress me. This is probably because I had a fairly impoverished childhood, and my own ancestors lived through the great famine of the 1840's, when foraging for food was far more important than sightseeing. It is perhaps for these reasons that I like to be assured that there is food about, and I am always happier when food is nearby.

Of course, there are plenty of fish in the sea – as the old saying goes – but one seldom sees those fishes. I have gone out into the sea to depths of nearly five feet and I have never encountered a single fish in these ventures. I remember on one occasion in late September when I happened to be by the sea, and I spotted a kind of rippling away out from shore. This rippling was, or seemed to be, about six or seven yards wide and mostly dark-coloured – a bit like a roadway. This 'roadway' was fast approaching the shore, so I watched intently as it advanced. The rippling effect on the water was like a squadron of mad motorcyclists roaring along the sea-bed underwater, but then, just as they got to the shore, they all swung around together as if to return into the sea, but it seems they took the turn a bit too sharp because at that point, some wildly-flapping fish were thrown up and out, and onto the sandy shore. It was only then I realised that the phenomenon I had first sighted away out to sea, was in fact a very large gathering of fish engaged in some kind of a race. Apparently, this exercise was not so rare along this stretch of coast, for there were boys on hand with buckets to catch those ill-fated fish. Later that evening, fish was being offered by the bucketful at a very cheap rate.

I must say that even though I was impressed by the vast numbers of fish that lie mostly-unseen in the sea, it is the sight of livestock grazing on lush green grass that reassures me that food is available, and is near at hand. What reassures me even more though, is the sight of straight rows of root-crops standing like trained soldiers shoulder-to-shoulder. I have often wondered why it is that I do not share this great admiration for rocky hills and brown heather with most of my fellows? Even when the heather is in full bloom it suggests nothing more to me than it would be the makings of a good "besom". One sight I shall never forget is when enterprising people in the County of Waterford had managed to get potatoes and carrots to grow on top of a rocky hilltop. The sight of tons of carrots and potatoes being conveyed by trailer down the hill en route to the market was a sight that I truly cherished. That, for me, was real excitement, and was scenery worth remembering.

I have since concluded that my early training on the land and the lessons it taught me might be the reason why I cannot truly enjoy 'the wild mountain scenery' like so many of my fellow citizens. In those days, I was close to the land and to the animals we reared. Mountains and heather were just the backdrop to the daily workings on the farm. I remember as a boy watching a single grain of oats grow up green and lush like grass, later turning a delightful golden yellow. When the head of this single stalk of oats had ripened fully I counted a hundred grains that had been produced from one single grain. A single potato sown properly in decent ground almost invariably produced ten or twelve more potatoes.

These miracles of nature have had a lasting impression on me. I learned at an early age that if these seeds were not planted in good ground these miracles would not happen. Even on good ground, the soil must be properly tilled, and by keeping the furrows straight, you ensure that all of the soil is tilled and that every square inch of the land is used.

Equally, I also know that if you turn out a cow that consistently produces five gallons of milk each day, she might barely be able to produce a half gallon if she is left browsing on that lovely purple heather.

12

In The Early Morning

IT IS NEARLY sixty years since I travelled the road from Bruff to Swinford by bike. As a cyclist, I always assume I will be heading into the wind, so I would leave home at ten minutes before seven in the morning, allowing myself one hour and ten minutes to cycle the ten-mile journey to Swinford. I did this trip for over a year and I do not remember ever getting wet, although I covered the whole of one winter and never missed a day at work.

The road is open and bleak for most of the way and the only hill that I walked was the hill in the town of Kilkelly. I used to dismount opposite Andy Egan's Butcher Shop and then walk up as far as the entrance gate into the old Garda Station. There, I would mount my machine again and put my head down and then pedal furiously for all I was worth.

Sometimes in the silence of the morning I would hear contented citizens snoring away as I crept silently by. It gave me a good feeling to be up-and-about earning my bread-and-butter while others were simply dreaming of ways of making money. But I was ever-cautious about making noise as I went through the town, because the people of Kilkelly treasured their peace and quiet – something that was jealously guarded by the townsfolk.

I recall an incident where a few interlopers from outlying areas were let out of a Licensed Premises within the town at about 2am. There was a group of five men in their early sixties. They were feeling in good form, but since they were all friends they were not inclined to fight amongst themselves, and there was nobody else about with whom they could do battle, so they decided to have a race. The prize was that each man would buy the winner a pint of stout. One of the group was wearing a new pair of clogs. They decided to walk up the town quietly and start at the junction of the Swinford Road, and the first man at the bridge was to be the winner. Coming down the hill at Lydon's they were all abreast, but then some of them pulled back so that 'galloping clog-man' was first past the winning-post.

Next morning some of the elders of the town paraded with sleep in their eyes up to the Garda Station complaining that there were horses galloping up and down the town all night. The law officers knew their district and could vouch that all of the local people kept their horses indoors during the winter nights. However, some less-privileged citizens who had little shelter for their families, and none at all for their horses were encamped nearby. The Gardaí duly made enquiries from these itinerant horse-owners, who pointed out quite indignantly, that none of *their* horses were shod, and shur wasn't it the case that the people in Kilkelly were so very sure that the horses they had heard, definitely had shoes on!?

As I pedalled easily and slowly out the Swinford Road, I took note that Kilkelly town had grown by about two houses since my younger days. There was now no clerk to note the time of my arrival in Swinford, for I was not really going anywhere except cycling easily along, and I was therefore in no great hurry. Some of the older houses had gone into disrepair and were apparently unoccupied. I noted the wide stone walls surrounding these small fields of less than an acre in most cases. I could picture the tough men who dug up the rocks and smashed them into pieces small enough to be carried and disposed of, into the great walls.

I was thinking as I sailed along that if the people who worked these fields had a choice they would have selected more productive land where food could be grown more easily. But strangers had arrived with big armies and guns, and they stole the good land from these hardworking people, who then wandered about until they found another place to settle. Invariably, that was on poorer, marginal land, but sometimes they were able to improve even those coarse lands, before the strangers came and took that too.

The land where these displaced people finally settled could not produce enough food to feed a family, but at least it was a nest that they could call home. From here, they worked for local property owners or for shopkeepers who could afford to pay them. Many went to England, where their love of the land found them working on English farms. Most English farms had a warm welcome for the worker from Kilkelly, who always did a solid day's work. English farmers even turned away their own people so as to reserve jobs for the Paddies.

Meanwhile, wives and children struggled at home. They were trying to do men's work. It was common for the women to get up before daybreak to spray the potatoes or sometimes to cut turf. These tasks were normally the exclusive preserve of the men. There were even occasional cases where the man did not return home for Christmas, or indeed did not return at all, until he had qualified for the old-age pension.

Indeed, it was an unsatisfactory arrangement even in the best-organised families. In the fifties and sixties, the women went across to England to work in factories, where nature would take its course. By the time they got married, they were familiar with the way of life in England. Families lived close to where the husband worked, and so the children went to the local schools, and consequently became English and lost their loyalty to the old sod.

The poor seasonal workers who went back and forth to England every year of necessity, were far more loyal to their native country than many of those at home who lived in much more privileged conditions. Yet it was from these priveleged classes that many Irish policital leaders emerged.

I have read many of the biographies of theses 'more privileged people' especially those who took a leadership role in Ireland. When you read of the 'hardships' that they suffered, your heart would bleed for them. Sometimes they had to cycle up to three miles to get to the secondary school, or ride on a bus for over twenty minutes as they went into the university. Often, their families suffered such deprivation that they had to resort to sowing vegetables in an area that was previously used for a tennis court. In one case the times were

73

so hard that they had to let one of their gardeners go. Imagine that! Very few of these privileged classes could understand the Mayo man who left school at fourteen, and went across to England in a cattle boat to work there for the rest of his life.

As I cycled along the bleak road, I noted that there were acres of ground where no house had been built, and no appearance of any attempt ever having been made to reclaim the land. Two delightful-looking little lakes were situated each side of the road. I stopped and I looked across the peaceful scene, and I could see that if the ground was smoothed out, and use was made out of the picturesque lakes, the place could be made into a top-notch golf course. A golf course is I know, a playground for the rich. I have never played golf myself, for when I was growing up the conventional wisdom was that if you got an opportunity to rest you should take it, for when the day was fine, you would not have any opportunity for resting.

I can recall now, that this road has not changed since I used to cycle to work all of those years ago. I think about my dream of having a golf course. It would draw people with clout into this part of the country, and they might want to settle and bring some of their prosperity along with them. I am reminded of a man who lived in these parts once, who had remained on in England and did not return until he qualified for the old age pension. He had always sent money home, but his wife was a bit suspicious and did not fully believe him when he told her some story of why he hadn't been able to come home all these years, like the other men in the village had. One night he took a few drinks and in the course of the night, in bed, he mentioned the name, "Dolly".

"It was only a dream. " He told his wife.

The wife was having none of it! So she declared war, and the poor man got his raincoat and old suitcase and stood out on the road looking for a lift to the train station. The wife became a bit sorry for him then, and went out to the road and she shouted, and called him back.

"Sure Michelin a gra, t'was only a drame".

———

74

Further down the road I remembered a farmhouse to which myself and half-a-dozen other boys of my own age went clumaireacht.[1] This was a custom in our part of the country, where young men disguised themselves with ropes of straw tied about their bodies, and visited the house where a wedding was taking place. We danced around the floor for a while and then we were offered the usual glasses of stout. All six of us were at the time members of the total-abstinence Pioneer Association. The house seems to have prospered, and so I hope that we brought them good luck.

---

[1] *Strawboys.*

13

The Hills Far Away

THE FIRST LANDSCAPE that my young eyes focused upon was the blue pinnacle of Cruach Padraig. This was directly west from where I used to live. Later on, I became familiar with the great hulk of the Neifin Mountain. I could see these sights at the lower end of the sky, but I had no idea that they were real, that is, in the sense that one could travel westwards and climb up the side of these mountains, and that it was even possible to stand on the top and look at the whole world. The top of Cruach Padraig was so pointed—or so it looked—that I was in some doubt that a person could balance on a perch so tiny. Later on I was shown the Twelve Pins to the south and the Ox Mountains to the north.

There was another mountain closer to us, but we did not dignify it with the title 'mountain'. We just referred to it as,"the hills beyond Kiltimagh". We spent quite a while studying this far-off sight, never actually climbing it or indeed even going close enough to be able to look up at it from the bottom. We would just lie up against the side of a mossy clay fence, resting ourselves after some task on the land, and my father would tilt the peak of his cap down over his nose and then peer westward at the hills beyond Kiltimagh. To me these distant hills seemed like a great reek of turf upon which someone had spread a patchwork quilt.

Father would point out that the seams on the quilt were really fences that had been built long ago by the people who farmed this elevated place. We would start our tour on the southern end of the hill and you could see a low hedge climbing northwards almost to the top. Here and there, you could see an occasional white dot which father told us were whitewashed stone houses. I got the impression that these houses must have been very small.

The first time I went to Castlebar, I had the opportunity for a closer view. The road to Castlebar passes close to the "low hedge" that I had been looking at for years. However, on closer inspection I could see that instead of a hedge, it was in fact a row of proud beech trees that must have been at least thirty feet high. It felt good to stand at the foot of this hill and look all the way up and see the whitewashed houses that seemed to go right up to the summit. Many of the little fields were a deep green, and others had crops of potatoes and oats that were ripening at the time. For me to just look up along this steep, rising hill, and see what bone and muscle had made of a once-barren piece of a mountain, was indeed a privilege.

Some years later, I was engaged as a vagabond labourer working along this area. I got to know the people. They are deep-thinking, much travelled and very learned folk. They did their travelling not to finishing schools or to exclusive universities to gain 'experience of life' as some of their more privileged neighbours did, but they travelled to get money from the sweat of their brows. They all seemed to be good-looking and the picture of health. I am reminded of an incident told of a similar type of people in the mountains in Co Cavan. Oddly enough, the people in that story were of the protestant religion. Their Pastor once paid a visit to a family of his flock. The lady of the house met him and bade him welcome. A few of the children came in to the house to see the visitor, and he remarked on their healthy good looks.

Later, the man of the house came in and the Pastor had the same thing to say to him. Manners dictated to the humble folk not to dwell on their own good fortune, but the visitor kept on talking on the comeliness of the children. "My wife and I have been trying to have children for the past ten years," said the Vicar, ". . but we have failed. We have been to Doctors in Dublin and London and even they cannot help. You have probably never visited a Doctor. . and just look at your lovely children! It must be the clear air!"

"You could be right there," said they both. They agreed that the wife of the Pastor would visit the cottage for a period, to take in some of that clear air. Realising all of the chores that his wife did around the Church, the Pastor wanted to limit her visit to as short a time as possible.

"How long do you consider she should remain?"

"Ah I would not be able to say. "

"Come come, my man, we are all men of the world!" said the Pastor masterfully.

"Well," said the man of the house cautiously. "If I was in good form, you could have her home again with you in the evening. "

I have often noticed that close beside where people are forced to scrape a living out of marginal land, there is usually rich fertile land not far away. It seems the case in this area too, for there are walled estates wherein privileged people used to live. Around these estates, trees were planted and grew well, throwing a great shadow along the edge of the road. I heard an old neighbour once tell of an experience that he had coming from Castlebar late one night. He had driven to Castlebar on a horse and sidecar and had spent a whole week in Court. By late Friday, he had succeeded in his appeal and was anxious to get home. The local farmer with whom he had lodged advised him against travelling that evening, because of the danger of being robbed.

The man was most anxious to get home however, and so he insisted he must go. The local farmer provided him with a stout stick, which he said was the least he could do, and then he advised the man to make sure that he sat on the 'wrong' side of the cart as well. Apparently, drivers were only supposed to sit on one particular side. So, the man set out on his journey and was going along at a good ol' pace, when from under the trees he heard some noise and saw a brawny man rush out of the darkness and try to grab his legs to pull him off the cart, but no legs were there! The driver then lashed out with his stick and caught the robber full on the shoulder, but the robber recovered and was coming for him now on the other side!But the wise old horse seemed to perceive the danger, and picked up quickly and moved on – and so the man escaped to tell the tale.

Having now seen this hill at close quarters, it made the viewing from afar more interesting. As the crow flies, the distance cannot be more than eight miles from our fields to these hills. We used to claim that we'd know when a crow was flying to Kiltimagh, as she'd have brought her dinner with her. We were careful not to crack this joke in the presence of the folks from around Kiltimagh, for they are a warlike lot and some of them might not take kindly to slights of that nature.

From different parts of our land, the view might be better to the north or the south or the east. There was one elevated little field where there was a good view of the east. The nearby hills obscured our view far away and it was not worth straining your eyes anyway, just to look at something that you saw every Sunday on the way to Mass. Father had a good knowledge of the hills north or south all the way to the horizon, for he used to tell of walking up there to find a spreesome six or seven miles away. In those days, before the passing of *the Dance Halls Act of 1927*, young men used to wander about the countryside at night in search of a spree. The admission to such places was free, but if you did not excel either at music or at dancing your welcome would not be so cordial – and probably would not last too long. Father and most of his pals seemed to be content to walk for hours and then just peep in the windows for a little while, before they set off again for home.

When I was young, I used to dream that one day I would be able to get a house away up on those hills beyond Kiltimagh, and face it into the rising sun and so have a great light that would be seen from our own fields. I thought that I might even be able to give signals to my old neighbours. But that was of course, before the mobile phone was even dreamt of.

Neiphin Beg

79

14

The Long Road to Claremorris

A S I FACED up the road to Claremorris, the memory of the first time I visited that town became fresh in my memory. I had gone back and over to England at least three times, and so I had been through Dublin. I had lived in cities in England for most of a year. Claremorris was only ten miles away from my home, but I had never set a foot in the place. I just never seemed to have any business to transact in Claremorris and so I had never been there. I could not tell my work colleagues that I was so backward of course, so one night as we sat around the fire at home, I announced to the family that I was going to Claremorris on the following morning.

"What are ye going to do in Claremorris?"

"Nothing. I just want to have a look at the place. "

"There's not much of it, to see. "

To fully enjoy the memory of my first visit I take the old road to Knock, and from there I enjoy the smooth, level roads that we all enjoy these days. I knew the old road to Knock and I could read the new signposts to Claremorris, and anyway, they said it was a straight road all the way. I was familiar with the narrow, damp little fields along the road as far as Knock. The green after-grass was growing up around rolled-up bales of grass that huddled close together in the corners of the fields. Long spikes of rushes were sprouting up as of old, much faster than the after-grass. Rushes seemed to be a favourite crop all along these little fields near the road.

Near the village of Knock there were a few green hills. I was thinking to myself that for some reason, people with 'influence' had kept far away from Knock as I could not see many mansions along the route. My own people on my father's side and on my mother's side all hailed from around these impoverished little fields. They say that all people are equal before God. To avoid any doubt about this, God sent his messengers to Knock. The people with power and money refused to believe that such a place as Knock would be singled out for such honour. It took the Pope himself to come and kneel at the grotto before they were convinced.

I called into the church and said a prayer for all of my relatives, most of whom are already peacefully resting, waiting for Gabriel's bugle call. I have always felt that the little old church in Knock is a place where God is close.

Out on the road again I began to climb up hills, observing that the land was drier here, with a noted absence of rushes. This was the sort of land the old British invaders liked. They would drive the natives off this fertile land at bayonet-point, and out into the bog. Their army remained for a while until big houses were built for the gentry, as well as cottages to house their servants. These servants acted as a local defence regiment whenever the army was required elsewhere. Soon, they had a few of the natives tamed, and in a second generation some of these natives were so well trained and tamed, that like the Irish Wolfhounds of old they would fight to the very end, on behalf of their English masters.

As I rode along I could trace some of the big houses with some of them still functioning. Many of the descendants of those 'planters' are now leading members of our society, and some have even become members of the Catholic faith. There was a time however, when it was profitable to be a Protestant. If a Catholic had any land, his Protestant neighbour was entitled by law to take it from him. A substantial farmer in Roscommon got wind that his Protestant neighbour was seeking to take his land from him.

The Catholic farmer immediately took lessons on Protestantism. At the time, a Protestant Bishop was attached to Castlerea. After this farmer had been some time under instruction, he was examined by the Bishop and certified as competent. The Bishop organised a party to which all the local gentry were invited. Included at the party was the man who had applied for his neighbours land. "Tell me," asked the Bishop, "What motivated you to change your religion?"

The farmer was silent for a moment and then he gave a slow wink to him who tried to take his land, and then he answered.

"Fifteen hundred acres, of the best land, in the County of Roscommon."

When I reached Claremorris I stood in the square and I deduced that it must have been here that the famous Horse Fair was held. It seemed a small area to have been the site of such renowned fairs. I recalled the time my father sold our Black Mare at the Claremorris Fair, in the month of July. I was about five years of age at the time, and would not be going with him. So, the evening before the fair my father put me astride the mare for the last time. I remember that my short legs could not grip on her broad back. So I held on for dear life, onto her coarse mane as father led her gently through the field.

He sold the mare the next day and it must have had a big impression on him, for he seemed to love talking of his experiences on that day. He sold the mare to a well-dressed horse dealer from the North of Ireland. After the deal was done, the buyer stood back and looked over the mare again and he remarked that she was indeed a noble-looking beast. Then, the usual good-natured banter would begin.

"I bet you drove her hard, on the way to the fair. " He said.

"She trotted every inch on the way a good ten miles, and I cycled along by her just holding the halter." Replied Father.

"She is a bit swollen to the front. I'd say her heart is not too good! But, I buy to sell again."

As the two men stood beside the mare, the local Canon came along. This was the local senior cleric, a red-faced heavy man with rings of flesh coming out from under his collar. An imposing figure, he made it his personal business to oversee all of the goings-on, and had no qualms about interfering where he may not be welcome. He was in the odd habit of carrying a walking stick by the ferrule end, with the curled end on the ground.

He inserted himself into the exchange, addressing the smartly-dressed dealer while ignoring my father. "Can you make anything of *them*?" asked the Canon. The implication was clear. The dealer seemed to feel the slight to my father and he responded with typical northern fire. "I have been dealing with these people who come into this town to do business, and I have always found them honest decent people!"

At this stage, the Canon walked off brusquely, leaving the northern visitor with a very poor impression of our Catholic clergy. My father often said that if he had been a friendly stray dog instead of a poorly-dressed local, the Canon might have acknowledged him. Certainly, he would have shown a stray dog more respect.

The horse-dealer belonged to another faith. He said he would not have believed that a clergyman, even of his own faith, would have treated father so disrespectfully. My father and the generations before him had been loyal to their faith, and they had suffered great deprivations because of that loyalty. But my father's impoverishment was obvious to the Canon, and so he took it as licence to ignore him. If father had rearranged his cloth cap in the manner of some of the landed gentry and wore a trimmed beard with perhaps riding-breeches and leggings, the Canon would no-doubt have felt honoured to speak to such a fine man.

The other landmark which was of significance to me was the site of the Bacon Factory. I cycled out the road to look up at it, for it is up on a hill. This was once the site of a British Army Camp where these worthies could look down on all. It was a long way to bring pigs up the hills for ten miles. Some people used to convey one or two pigs in a donkey and cart. My father always used the horse and cart, but this too was a bit of a hazard, for pigs are an awkward cargo. Horses, unless they are old and weak, resent pigs being anywhere near them.

As I cycled past the Church I thought of the red-faced Canon again, and how rude he was to my father. He did this because he could. People accepted this sort of arrogance from those in authority. The Canon had clearly judged my father to be a struggling small farmer who, like all poor folk, was well-conditioned into accepting a slap with the master's stick, or a disrespectful put-down every time they met one of their 'betters'. This was probably considered to be good social policy by the gentry, so as to keep the peasantry under control.

In those days, the gentry kept a good table and it was customary to invite the leaders of the dominant religion to partake in their celebrations. Even if they were a bit impoverished, being a member of the gentry allowed them to have a certain self-confidence, and they would not tolerate insults from any quarter. I think that we have been learning a bit too much from them. All the same, he who speaks with a spud in his mouth is still likely to get a better hearing.

Fair Day in Ballyhaunis c.1950

15

A Visit to Ballyhaunis

YOU COULD SURVIVE on the goods and services that were available locally, but if you needed a real variety, Ballyhaunis was the place to go. Any equipment required for use on the land like a plough or a mowing-machine could be bought in the town of Ballyhaunis. Needless to say all of the parts for any piece of equipment needed on the farm were there in plenty. Nearly anything that was made of wood or iron could be bought in Ballyhaunis. On fair days and occasionally on market days too, churns would be there, ready for use.

I remember seeing the cooper himself standing on the square, demonstrating how well put-together his churns were. He would lift a churn up over his head and let it drop with a loud bang down on to the concrete on the edge of the square. I suppose he often sold churns to people attracted by his compelling salesmanship, but not everybody needed to buy a churn or, perhaps if they did, they might not have the money to pay the cooper.

He certainly added to the spectacle of the fairs and markets, for these were places of fun and amusement where craftsmen displayed their skills, and artisans showed their wares. Coopers belonged to a unique breed of craftsmen who were always prepared to entertain their customers, and often, an entourage of supporters would follow them about. One evening the cooper left his wares at the market place and went into a drapery shop. The proprietor himself came out to serve him.

"I want a shirt. "

"What sort of a shirt? Is it one with a collar attached – or one with separate collars?"

"I don't know. I just want a shirt. "

"Perhaps something like the one you are wearing?"

"Ah no, I want a clean one!"

Though it was a relatively small town, there were many entertaining characters living in the town, or in the townlands adjacent thereto. There were strong men who would lie on the road on top of broken glass and invite the heaviest men at the fair to stand on their chest.

I remember the first time that I cycled up to Ballyhaunis. I was familiar with the road as far as Aghamore for I went along this road every week to Mass. I had also been to Ballyhaunis Fair driving cattle, taking the shortest route up the back-road and out onto Doctor's Road. Now that I was on the bicycle, I was advised to go the longer way, as these roads were tarred at the time. I remember the hills up through Mountain and then it was downhill, along by Castle and Coolnaha Townlands, and then I swung right up by the Golf Course. I knew I was on the right road when I saw the entrance to the Golf Course. It was not that I was familiar with the game, but I had seen the golf clubs in the back of a car driven by a shopkeeper from Kilkelly. I got a simplified version of the game of golf as, "a game played by fat old men. "

I noted that the land became poor here, and there was a lake visible on my left. I fancied that it might not be too far for me to travel if there was any fish in it. I was figuring that the Glore River must have started in that lake. I often dreamt of going fishing, although up to that point I had never caught a fish. I had seen a boat out fishing once on the Cloughwally Lake – it belonged to Dr Lyons in Kilkelly. I still dream of going fishing but have never seriously tried it – at least, not yet. So there I was, daydreaming and cycling along and before I knew it, I was close to the town.

I remembered my first ever visit to Ballyhaunis. As I approached the town, a group of about five or six boys of school-leaving age were half-way across the road, and I had to slow down to get past them. On seeing that I was about their own age, they caught a hold of the carrier of my bicycle and made me dismount. A small red-headed fellow challenged me to show why I had come up to their town? I had no answer to this question, and so I was silent.

"Can you fight?" They asked me, and I said that I could, "A bit".

Then they all laughed at me. Whether it was my accent, or the confused expression on my face, I did not know.

A tall pale-faced fellow danced out on the road in front of me and challenged me to take him on. I was not particularly fond of fighting, but there seemed to be no way out but to have a go. So I left my bicycle a few yards on the town side of the scene, and I moved reluctantly out on to the centre of the road. The other contestant and I stood looking at each other, and then the red-headed fellow called the first man to, "Leave a wet finger on him!" That started it, and we began flailing away at each other for all we were worth.

I had no boxing skills, so I just swung my fists at my opponent, and hoped that if he hit me that I would not feel much pain. Then we got into a clinch, and I knew that I had good strength in my hands and arms. I got a grip on my man just above the elbow, where his arm was thin enough for me to get a right-good grip. Then he began to howl, and boy, did I put on the pressure. He began to bawl and cry then, and so his friends came in and separated us.

"Why don't you stand up and fight like a man!?" . . they all began to shout at me, and then they went ministering to their injured warrior. I saw my opportunity, and hopped on the bicycle and did not look back. Like the Three Wise Men from the East in the Bible, I took a different route home. I had no problems on that occasion, and nobody invited me out to fight. If they had, I expect that I'd have tried to talk my way out of any such encounter.

There was little difference in distance from our place to Ballyhaunis or Kiltimagh, but father favoured the fair in Kiltimagh. At the time, a train went from Kiltimagh into Pettigo in Co Donegal, and so farmers and cattle dealers from Northern Ireland used to come frequently to Kiltimagh Cattle Fair. The buyers who attended Ballyhaunis were mostly from the midlands and were more inclined to haggle. Often, they waited until it was late in the day to come to buy. By this time, the sellers were tired after the long day standing on the fairgreen, and so it was assumed that the stock might be more easily bought. The men from the north on the other hand, just came and looked at the stock and if they considered them suitable, they offered the full price with no haggling. They paid you as soon as the banks opened, and as soon as CIE had the wagons shunted, you put your stock on the train for Pettigo.

The cattle being sold in these fairs were known as "store cattle". These were cattle that had made their full growth in height, but were too thin yet for the beef industry. The buyers put these cattle out onto good pasture and in a few months time, they often doubled their weight.

After most of the business of buying and selling was completed, a more social aspect to the fair occurred. In the olden times, young ladies would come late to the fair, picking their steps through the slush and animal-droppings, and make their way in their pretty little shoes into the snugs. Snugs were cosy off-shoots from the main bar in the pubs; little nooks that sat maybe three or four at most, while the men stood apart at the bar sinking pints, smoking pipes and jawing about the day's business. A man with money in his pocket after selling a few cattle would visit some of these places, and buy drinks for some of his friends. A lady in the snug with her 'Pocket Book', well-full after ten or fifteen years in America, might just attract his attention.

Bill Naughton, Author

This might be the first contact, and then later in the week, a more businesslike approach might be made. The late Bill Naughton—a distinguished writer from Ballyhaunis—tells of his own mother's experiences at a fair in Kiltimagh. His mother hailed from Ballinacostello and that day, she was on the look-out for a husband. A man from Caher was nominated as a prospect, and she was happy enough to go ahead with the deal, but, then she saw him walking down the street with the clip on the back of his boots sticking out. She said that she could never marry a man who wore his boots like that! Later, she would marry a man who worked as a shop-boy in Ballyhaunis. His experience with the public had taught him how to dress himself properly.

The second-hand clothes-sellers had a portable drapery shop on the street. These were much more colourful individuals than their more dignified colleagues inside the doors of their own shops. I remember one fellow who would take up a jacket and assert that it was once worn by the President of the United States. He had other garments previous worn by the King of Spain. The Duke of York seemed to be a particularly versatile fellow for he seemed to have jackets that would be a tight fit for our local diminutive blacksmith, and trousers that would be loose on our esteemed Parish Priest.

Many country people bought from these standings, for they also had suitable garments for doing rough farm-work. Swinford was a great town for the sale of second-hand clothes, which was just as well, because some people with a degree of snobbery would go off to a town where they wouldn't be known. Some well-to-do farmers for example would not like to be seen by their neighbours to be buying second-hand clothes. One fellow I knew well was of that disposition, and so he went to Swinford where he felt he would not be known. He was doing a deal for a second-hand topcoat, and the dealer was not getting it all his own way.

"Sure I didn't come down here to buy a topcoat! I came down from Claremorris to buy a few cattle!"

Just as he was handing over the money, his next-door neighbour stepped forward and said.

"Aha, so you finally bought it, I see!"

———

In my time, we kept certain 'business' (that of meeting prospective romantic partners) completely separate from the business of the fair. We attended local dances of course, but the patrons we met there was not a subject to be discussed at a public fair. However, some of the older people still associated the fair with romance. One day I was assisting my father when an elderly man came up to look at our stock, and he admired our few cattle.

"Of course, ye have good land out there in Aghamore." Father accepted the compliment as it was intended as a personal compliment. Then the old fellow turned to me and said:

"I hear that you will soon be moving into our village?" This I knew, was a reference to a young lady with whom I had walked part of the way home, but it was *not* something I wanted debated amongst old men at a public fair! I was speechless, and so I walked off with a burning red face.

Romantic affairs were not subjects that I ever debated with my father, and fair play to him, he never ever mentioned this exchange, although I am sure that he was amused.

16

Clocking-Hens

YEARS AGO, AT the right time of year, there was hardly a house in the whole parish where the guttural sound of the clucking-hen would not be heard. For some reason that I cannot explain, the adult female hen changes its accent 'in season' when the urge towards motherhood comes upon her. I have known of a few females of the human species, who change their accents as soon as they set foot on the boat to Hollyhead. In their case, this change of sound becomes permanent, but the hens at home revert back to their characteristic high-pitched accents as soon as the seasons change.

For the poultry manager, the first visible manifestation of this urge to hatching is when a number of hens do not join their sisters as usual in romping about the farmyard. Instead, they congregate about the cow byres and attempt to make nests in the broken hay and dust left over after foddering the cows. Despite the absence of amorous cockerels, these birds are nevertheless intent on brooding and will sit, most determinedly, all day and every day, on any and all eggs they can beg, borrow or steal, or upon those they lay themselves, and all while clocking contentedly away. But if hatching hens were not required that year, it was found useful at this point to chase them off with the dog. A few such panicked runs would usually takeaway the immediate desire to start a new family – at least, not in such a hazardous place.

In the olden times there was nearly always a demand for a few clocking-hens. In the days before the incubator was widespread, hens were used to hatch out eggs of her own species as well as those of ducks, turkeys and geese. There was good co-operation between the various managers of poultry farms. One farm might have too many clocking-hens and another farm might not have enough. There were no formal arrangements, but the parties often exchanged information on their way home from Mass of a Sunday.

I knew one enterprising woman who could conscript any hen in off the street and set her up as a clocking hen. She simply caught any hen at all, but preferred big hens or older ones whose laying days were over, and who could cover more day-old chicks or eggs. Once the hen was captured, it was chained to the leg of the kitchen table with a bootlace and kept there for a day or two. Sometimes the hen might be a bit stubborn and would refuse to cluck. Then, if day-old chicks were let loose with her, she might follow them with intent to assault or kill them. The solution was to take a lighted sod of turf and blow it with your breath until it glowed red, and then push the hen's beak into the flames. This treatment was only used as a last resort, but was usually enough to change the tune of the most uncooperative hens.

I should point out that the affairs of clocking-hens were invariably dealt with by the most senior woman in the household. Any boy who showed open interest in clocking-hens ran the serious risk of being regarded as a sissy. Despite this knowledge, I must admit that I could not resist having an occasional peep at the clockers in confinement, and I often saw them perched on the rail under the kitchen table.

It may well be the case now that hens have forgotten how to cluck, and, if some of the poultry farms are having difficulties in getting them to revert to the ways of nature, they might try chaining them back to the leg of the dining-room table for a few days. Lighted sods of turf might be in short supply these days, but perhaps a large candle or, in a pinch, a cigarette lighter may suffice. As I have already mentioned, I have only a rudimentary knowledge of the poultry industry. The older experts in this field did not unfortunately, commit to writing down detailed accounts of their experiences, so many of the finer points of hen-keeping may already be lost to us. As in so many other aspects of rural life here in Ireland, we are left mostly reliant on accounts by practitioners of the old ways,from other lands. Third level colleges have access to these sources of course, but these academic sources may lack the kind of homely touches that are so essential for success.

17

The Electric Spade

IT SEEMED THAT every time that my mother came home from the local shop, she had news of yet another neighbour leaving for England. For hundreds of years people had been leaving for either England or America, but these times it seemed everybody was leaving. My father would hear this news with an air of sadness, and he would pull out a chair from the end of the table and heave a deep sigh and say, "Soon they will all have cleared out. "I was about six or seven years of age at the time, and even I felt the sadness.

There was money to be had in plenty trying to rebuild England after the destruction of the Second World War. Girls were replacing the young men killed in action, and were now taking their places working in British plants and factories. The young men of Ireland were also engaged in re-building English towns and cities. The Irish had been doing this type of work for two or three generations – often sending the best and the brightest of the local community to Britain. The difference now was that even the old, and the young, and the weak, and the maimed were leaving for foreign shores.

The English were a resourceful people in those days, and generally found jobs to suit varied talents. One man I knew who was too incapacitated to make a living out of his own land, found a job where he was allowed to sit down all day peeling potatoes. Another claimed he had a job shaving gooseberries in a jam factory. This would have been considered a very suitable job for such a smart fellow at the time. Occasionally, there were miscalculations however, and a man in his late sixties was put wheeling barrows of concrete across a narrow unstable plank. When the man looked down over ten feet into a pool of filthy water he froze, scared stiff. There was a line of other men following him and so they too, were all held up.

The young men on the job began to jeer him. Some were his neighbours from home, but they had become coarse and vulgar from rough living and the consumption of copious quantities of beer. They showed no respect for their old neighbour who would have been much more privileged than they were, at home. They began to jibe, using the lingo of the northern cattle-dealers when they encouraged drovers to get stubborn cattle onto the wagons in Kiltimagh.

"Close up on em, and give it plenty of the sthick, and twist its tail!"

These cruel words did not move the elderly man on, who was thereafter stuck solidly to the ground. Finally, some sensible foreman took control and he got a more suitable job for the old workman. Many of these wild young men earned a great deal of money and they spent it liberally, so that all that they had after a lifetime of hardship was ill-health and broken bones.

Looking back to those days, it seems to me now that very little work was going on at home. The talk was always about 'the big money' that was being earned in England. The parents of these young men were competing with each other about which of their children earned the most. Around our parish at that time, men were doing heavy digging for two shillings a day; which would work out at twelve shillings a week. There was 20 shillings to a pound. Men in England were getting ten pounds a week doing the same kind of work.

One neighbouring woman used to visit our house showing the cheques that she had received from her sons. These cheques were frequently over a hundred pounds. I can still see her sad, tear-stained face, as she recounted the long hours that her boys worked,". . the poor things!" Then she would recall how hard things had been when her young boys were growing up. She would turn to me and note how quickly I was growing up too, and that soon, I too would be off.

Money was coming to her fast now, but she would spend it as fast as it came. Not everybody wasted their money though, and many made good and picked up useful skills that stood to them later on, for use on the land. Those who spent as they earned usually had stories to share and some had great storytelling skills to tell of their vagabond days. Once, I heard a man telling of how they used to roast a hen on the head of a shovel. We had hens in plenty at the time, so I considered a culinary experiment, but on mature reflection, I decided against it.

Many Irish workmen were employed building air-raid shelters before the war. After the war was over, these very same men were employed in knocking them down again. Rarely would you get a description of these works, but one night an elderly fellow began to tell how they set about their work of knocking down an air-raid shelter. For this job they were supplied with what he called 'an electric spade'. Now, all of his listeners knew what a spade was of course, but 'an electric spade'? Well now, that was something else to be hearing about!

For the purpose of his explanation, he took possession of the tongs from the hearth. He got down on his knees on the floor at the end of the kitchen table. He pushed out one leg of the tongs onto the stone floor. Then he said, "Press Thumb!" and he put his thumb on the knob of the tongs while tapping the tongs on the floor and verbalising the words, "Diddle-diddle, diddle-diddle, diddle-diddle... "

"Remove thumb!" says he, and there was silence. Then he pressed his thumb down again and began tapping the tongs on the floor again, saying,"..diddle-diddle, diddle-diddle, diddle-diddle.." At this point there was a spontaneous burst of laughter from about three of his younger listeners.

Immediately he got up off the floor and approached his youthful listeners and addressed them as follows.

"What are you laughing at!?"

Since no reply was forthcoming he repeated his question in a louder and more sombre tone.

There was complete silence then, and so he resumed his seat by the fireside, and said no more.

I had often wondered what an electric spade would look like. Then one day as I was passing along the road I came upon a group of workmen putting down pipes for water. Suddenly someone pressed their thumb on the starter of the jackhammer, and there it was! "Diddle-diddle, diddle-diddle, diddle-diddle!" I burst out laughing and I kept laughing as I walked along the road.

18

Haymaking

IN SO FAR as I was involved, the preparations for haymaking were the least-demanding of all of the annual chores. In the early spring we put out as much top-dressing of farmyard manure as we could spare. In addition to this, we would spread about two hundredweight of artificial manure on each acre. We'd run around and pick up the stones and any other encumbrances that had mysteriously gotten into the meadow while it was being grazed during the winter.

Often enough, farm animals had made gaps in the fences during their occupation, and these had to be mended. Last of all, the main entrance-gap had to be closed off. In our case, we cut a fairly tall thorn-bush and dragged it into the entrance-gap and filled in any other weak spots with smaller bushes. In those days very few farmers had gates to their fields. Occasionally a man might use a sheet of galvanised iron or a few strands of barbedwire tied to two stakes as a makeshift gate, so as to prevent any unwanted intrusion to the meadow.

We left the rest to God, to send us—(if it were possible)—rain on the meadow, and sunshine on the tillage-fields and on the bog. In the first week of July we opened the main gap and began cutting the meadow. In the normal way, we reserved about seven acres of land to be cut for hay. My father would mow all of this with a hand-held scythe. He was a low-sized man of powerful build, and so he was, as you might say, designed for mowing with a scythe.

During any wet days at the end of June, father would make some preparations for the hay. First of all he would rig up the scythe and give the blade a good sanding. He used to flatten stout short nails, and hammer these in around the scythe handles or "doirneens" as we used to call them. The same remedy was used to tighten the heel of the scythe. He had his own long-handled pitchfork and the fork itself was sharp and shiny with the handle polished a bright yellow. He also needed to provide implements for use by the younger members of the family. For months he used to have long, straight rods about an inch-and-a-half thick, of ash or laurel or sometimes hazel. These would be stored under the rafters in the shed to season, later to be used as handles for hay-forks. I never knew where he got the fork-heads but he always seemed to have a good supply on hand.

These fork-heads had long spikes that could be driven into one end of the handle. To give this part added strength and stability he used to cut about four inches off a tubular bar and fit it on top of the handle,before boring a hole to receive the thin spike of the fork-head, which he would then drive home. These tubular pieces were cut from the crossbar of an old bicycle. Usually of a damp evening, he would open the meadow and mow a few short curved swards.[1] Next day he would begin fairly early and keep moving along slowly. I would select the best of the new forks and I would begin to shake out the hay that was being cut. My aim was to try to cover over with hay, all of the area from which the grass had been cut. If the crop was light this was not easy. When he had cut about two acres of grass father would hang up his scythe on a nearby tree and would use a wooden rake to begin to 'turn' the hay that I had shaken out. When I say 'turning' it was not really turning, but raking the hay or grass into thin rows.

In showery weather these small rows would be made into what we called 'footcocks'. To make these small haycocks you gathered about a yard of the row using your foot to keep the collected hay against the rake. Then you reached forwards and pulled a few feet of the row up on top of the gathering you had made. These little cocks would witstand light rain and the centre of them would be drying, even when it was raining.

We would later gather up these little footcocks and build them into a larger fieldcock which allowed the hay to season a bit more, before it was carted into the haggard.[2] After these fieldcocks had stood for

_____
[1] *"Sward" – an upper layer of soil with short grass upon it.*

at least a few hours—or maybe on the following day—they would be trimmed down, and a hay-rope was was made to keep the cock from being unfurled by wind. I found it facinating to watch the skilled men pull out a few strands of hay and twirl it around their thumb and keep on pulling until enough of a rope had been made to go around the cock.

Father would keep on mowing until he had at least enough hay standing in fieldcocks to make a proper haystack in the garden. It took about one hundred fieldcocks to make a haystack. We usually had about three good-sized haystacks in the haggard. Making the haystack needed care and quite some skill. Our haystacks were usually built on the same site each year and so a circle of big stones was already in situation, but we always threw in a few extra branches of trees to keep the hay up off the ground. The great principle of haystack-building was to keep the centre of the haystack tightly-filled, so that if any moisture came on the outside it did not flow inwards. The vissicitudes of our weather required that you had to be resourcefulat times. I remember a few times that when the hay was considered to be too fresh or not fully dry, that we had to put a chimney into the haystack.

This was done as follows: Once you had the bottom layer of the stack set out, you filled a sack tightly with hay and set it right in the centre. Then, as you built the haystack upwards and outwards around it, you kept pulling up the sack bit-by-bit, leaving a neat vetilation-hole underneath. You repeated this action until you were close to the top. The sack was then pulled clear of the haystack and this new invisible 'chimney' was covered off with a good forkful of hay – taking care of course, that no hay fell back into the hole.

Bringing the hay into the haggard required a whole fine day – preferably a still day with not much of a breeze. We used a horse-and-cart, but a horse-cart is a very small foundation upon which to build a large load of hay. Very skilled men could do it, but I was only about seven years of age when I first attempted to do this, and so my efforts were not always praiseworthy. To assist me, father devised a method where he extended the width and length of the cart

---

[2] "Haggard"- a stackyard or enclosure on a farm for keeping hay

by about a foot on every side. Upon this broad structure father built the load from the ground-up, and I simply walked about on the hay to press it down a bit. If father built a good load then I got the credit for being a good loader, but if father built the load all to one side and it was in danger of falling or of overturninmg the cart, then I certainly got the blame for poor workmanship.

Before the winter set in, the haystacks were trimmed and the top of the stacks were usually capped off with a good coating of sedge-grass obtained in the bog. The sedge was believed not to be affected by the weather as much as good quality hay. When the time came to feed the hay to animals it was not taken off from the top, but instead it was cut with a hay-knife from the top down, taking out about a quarter of it in the first cut – just like a huge slice of cake, the height of three men. The next cut left just half of the stack and it was still stable. Once you began to cut out the third quarter though, it was a matter of being very careful, for at this stage the whole lot might tumble.

When the hay was being cut into sections the seeds of the saved grass often fell about the garden and little song-birds flew in from the fields to eat their fill. It was good to watch these shy little creatures as they flocked about the haystack, but they were suspicious of humans. They had good reason to be wary, especially of us younger boys. Whenever they were seen I would use a basin or a sieve to try to catch one or more of them. The idea I had, was to confine them to a small birdcage so that I could watch them up close or show them off to my friends.

A typical haystack

It was only when the weather was inclement and they could not get to their usual sources of food, that these birds ventured into the proximity of humans. Catching them required some planning. The idea was to prop up one side of the basin or sieve, with a short piece of a stick. You tied a long string or a woollen thread to the bottom of the stick and you concealed yourself in the half-cut hay stack.

Now, when you figured that a bird was under the trap you pulled the string and the basin (or sieve) was supposed to fall down and capture the creature. Sometimes you might get more than one bird if the basin or sieve was big enough. When you knew you had a captive, you got a big old coat and spread it all over thebasin and you inserted your hand underneath and felt around until you felt some hot, feathered little body. My experience was that mostly I had caught a tom-tit, and this aggressive little fellow will give a sharp nip with his beak causing the intrepid hunter to withdraw and retreat so suddenly, that all of his would-be prisoners, escaped.

19

Harvesting

THE PREPARATION FOR the harvest usually began early in the month of March. If a new piece of lea-land was to be added to our tillage land, the usual crop was oats. Local farmers in our area always liked to have lea-land ploughed as early in the spring as was possible. The idea was to disturb the pests that had made their home in the grass, and, before they had time to regroup the farmer would then harrow the ploughed land. Ploughed land needed to be given a light harrowing so that the oat seeds did not drop down between the ploughed sods, and be lost.

In some areas a special implement was used to scatter the seeds. This was known as a 'seed fiddle'. This modern contraption (at the time) flung out seeds in a constant pattern, depending on how fast the sower drew his bow through it. However, the farmers that I knew had no need for any such fancy implement. They just filled the seeds into a bucket and walked along taking fistfuls as they went, throwing the seed out in a circular fashion. The skill of these men needed no mechanical gauge, for they could apply the seed in exactly the way

The Seed Fiddle

that was required. These men had studied very closely how best to sow their crops. In some areas and especially when the farms were very small, they would sow the oat seeds thickly so that the straw that was left after the harvest was thin and light, and was usable for feeding the cattle.

I often saw my father counting the number of grains in a stalk of oats. He sowed his oats mostly for the grain, and had found from experience that oats that were scattered too thickly on the ground did not produce as much grain per head as if the seed was sown more sparsely. Thickly-sown seeds usually produced thin stalks, which were good for fodder but didn't produce great yeilds of corn or oats. But thinly-sown crops often yielded over a hundred big grains of oats in a single stalk. Whereas thickly-sown oats might not yield more than fifty grains. In which latter case, the straw would also have a similar lack of substance.

Sowing was not just a matter of scattering grains of oats or seeds on ploughed land. The ground had to be thoroughly harrowed, lengthways and crossways, and, if the seeds were not fully covered, then it was harrowed again until the grains were mostly invisible. But keen-eyed spectators observed from the tall trees nearby, and when the work was done the crows came along to have a feast. It was a tough fight between the farmer and the crows. Some farmers had shotguns, and others set up scarecrows in the form of 'an fear breaga' – or 'false men'. Each of these efforts had some effect, but the crows had their successes too.

The next task for the farmer was to pick up any loose stones that had been upturned with the cultivation, and then finally, the whole field had to rolled. This rolling pressed the seeds into the ground, and firmed-up the surface. Most farmers had a simple wooden roller comprising the stump of a tree into which twopins had been driven on each side to act as axles. These rollers were light, and often needed repairs due to their constant use. We used to borrow this implement from a neighbour, but one year the roller-owner was in bad humour and he refused to lend his machine, and so my father decided to make his own. He had on stores[1] a steel barrel that was too small to use for spraying the potatoes. The spray was made up to suit a forty-gallon barrel, but the steel barrel we had was only about half that size.

Still, it stood over four feet high, and so we made a round hole in the bottom of the barrel through which we pushed one end of the axle of a horse-cart. On the top of the barrel we fixed a stout piece of timber through which the other end of the axle protruded. Having checked that each end of the axle was centred and protruded evenly, we set thedevice upright with one end submerged into the ground by about

---

[1] "On stores" – stored away in a safe place while not being used.

a foot. The next task was to fill the barrel with a good rich mixture of concrete, and then wait for a week or two for the concrete to set. Now, we had a good roller of our own, but how to get this heavy contraption going? By digging away the soil alongside it was possible to knock the roller sideways and then just roll it out. In olden days this method was used to bury boulders that were too big to be moved.

We always had some rough timbers on stores, and so father made up a good strong frame which did duty with most of the neighbours for many years. Once the field was rolled, it was then time to close the main gap into the oat field. From time to time of a Sunday, father would climb in over the fence and walk about to check if his field of oats was doing well. Around the end of July he would welcome— at least in the field of oats—bright sunshine and frequent showers – as long as they were not too heavy.

On his inspections he would detect if any of the crop had lodged.[1] This might be a rare occasion for tantrums– as if his family could run in there and just hold up the oats!? This would be the first area to be cut when harvesting-time came. There was very little preparation for harvesting. The trusty scythe would be tightend-up, and the blade given a good sanding.

Two men was a useful team for harvesting, but in our case it was a case of one man and a boy. Father would mow the oats in against the standing crop, and I as a "taker out" moved backwards, working behind the mower well-away from the swinging scythe. You put your right hand in over the cut sward and over the freshly-cut crops, and took a pace backward as you scooped up this handful of cut oats. About three such lifts was enough to make an adequate sheaf. You carried this sheaf about three yards out and placed it on the ground with the grain facing inwards, towards the standing crop. If two men were engaged on this operation the "taker out" would also tie the sheaves. However the fact that these sheaves were left 'open' as it were, for most of the day meant that they got well-aired and dry with the sun.

---

[1] *"Lodging" – the bending-over of the stalks of grain crops, near the ground, making them difficult to harvest.*

The way we tied the sheaves was by standing behind the sheaf with the grain-end facing your right hand. With this hand, you took up about ten or twelve strands of corn into a small band. Then, lifting the main sheaf barely off the ground, you passed the cut-end of the band underneath the sheaf and grabbed it with your left hand. At the same time you caught the grain-end of the band between your left index-finger and thumb, thus encircling the main sheaf. You then gave the sheaf one full twist with your right hand and pushed the resulting knot in under the band itself. You then turned the sheaf down, so the knot was on the ground. Later, when you came to stooking (the next stage in the harvesting process) you took these sheaves two at-a-time under each arm so that the knots would be inside the standing stook.

In haymaking and in harvesting there were tried-and-tested methods which some followed in the firm belief that any sort of system makes for better efficency. But I have seen people tying sheaves of oats by picking up the sheaf on to their knees and then twisting the band until it was tight, before stacking them into stooks. This was a slower procedure that created a great lump under the band which often held moisture, and furthermore, sheaves that were tied in this manner often became loose as well.

Stooking was also done with a specific method. You picked two sheaves under each arm and placed them against each other on the ground, grain-end upwards, with two propping-up two in a standing A-frame. Then you added four more sheaves to this structure, and usually,then another four to that. That was twelve sheaves in each standing stook. They were stacked this way so that the grain-heads were well-ventilated and kept out of the reach of vermin. It was standard practice to form stook-rows about ten paces apart. These were always in straight lines. It looked smarter like that, and it also facilated carting home the harvest. You drove your cart between two of these rows, and so carting home was done in orderly fashion.

You could never get an early start at harvesting because you had to wait for the grain to dry, and during harvest time there was invariably a heavy morning dew. Around eleven o'clock was as early as you could begin. Working without delay and as fast as proper standards would allow,we used to cut and stack about a hundred stooks a day – or a few more if conditions were favourable. We always seemed to be stooking with the light of the moon.

Around two in the afternoon, my mother would place a white sheet on a thorn bush visible from the harvest field. This indicated that dinner was being served. I used to keep a sharp lookout for the blessed warning, for I seemed to be always hungry in those days. Around six o'clock,mother would arrive with a jug of tea and a few cuts of bread. Father would light his pipe and blue smoke would assend for a few minutes before we got back to work again.

Loading sheaves of corn on to a cart was somewhat easier than loading hay, but you still had to be on the watch, for sheaves of corn can be heavy too, especially if there is a full load. If the load was not equally stacked on each side for instance, or if front and rear was unbalanced, there was a real danger of serious accident because the whole lot could suddenly tumble over, taking horse and cart with it. The load only had to ride on the cart for a few minutes, but the stack of sheaves in the garden had to survive the whole of the winter.

The making of the stack of cornsheaves was serious work assigned only to senior staff, and this latter crept about on his knees about three feet in from the edge while he was building it. Like the haystack, it was of primary importance that the centre of the stack be kept well-filled. The shape taken by the butts of the sheaves while stooked, led to an inclination for the stack to become wider as it went upwards. So, when the stack was seven or eight feet high, the sheaves were then turned inwards so that the butts had the opposite inclination, making the ever growing monster-stack become narrower as it went upwards. When the sheaves were almost standing on their ends at the top of the stack, the stack-maker would pull-out a band from one of the sheaves and tie it right around the top of the stack, holding it secure in the same manner as a stook. Albeit a massive stook that was over 15 feet high.

Most of the farmers in our area would have up to twenty such stacks in the garden. Like the haystacks before them, these cornstacks now had to be made to look well, as well as be fit to throw off the rain and snow of winter. If any sheaf was protruding in an unsightly manner it might be cut off to become even with the others. Usually, a spade was used to stab the offending stack inwards so that the bigger stack took on that traditional, pretty shape of being narrow at the bottom and wide at the sceimheal (skivel) with a long, even roof.

Cornstack

To finish these stacks off for the winter, a single sheaf was scutched of all its grain and about two bands of straw was tied about half way down this sheaf. A stick, like a brush-handle was inserted firmly into the banded sheaf. In local paralance this was known as a "goggle". By now, the whole roof of the stack was thatched with additional straw that had been inserted well-into the sheaves at the top. When this work was completed the goggle-handle was pushed firmly down into the top of the stack. The top of the goggle-sheaf was was left sticking out and was then spread-out like a shawl down over the thatch. Long straw ropes were then circled around the stack starting at the skivel and going on up to meet the bands at the top of the stack. Pieces of willow-rods about two feet long were inserted here and there above the ropes to keep them from sliding upwards. Finally, the thatch was cut evenly all around at the skivel. Such stacks were indeed a fine work of art.

When the thatching programme was about to commence some sheaves were thrashed of their grain and all foreign matter was shaken out, so that nothing was left but straight wisps of straw. This thatching-material was also used for making straw ropes, known as 'súgán'. In our area, a woman or boy would twist the straw into shape while a more-qualified person remained by the main bundle feeding out straw evenly. The twister used a light stick of about eighteen inches long and when the first band of straw was doubled over it, would spin the stick much like the driver of a motor car spins a steering-wheel. As more straw was fed into the strands the twister would inch backwards, so that between them, a strong, even rope of about an inch-and-a-half thickness was being made. The length of each rope was at the discretion of the man doing the feeding. But approximately thirty feet was the standard length, which could be completed by an expert rope-maker in 10-15 minutes. Once they reached the right length, the twister stopped twisting, and the man at the other end would coil his end around his thumb before winding the rope into an oval shape around and under his elbow, about twice the size of a rugby ball. He wound this ball tightly pulling the twister towards him as he went, until finally, he tied off a knot and loosened the stick, handing it back to the twister to begin all over again.

20

Potatoes

OF ALL THE crops that have ever been grown in this country, the humble potato has the greatest association with us in good times, and in bad. Commonly known as 'praties' 'tatties' or 'spuds' we had been growing them here for about 250 years when the great famine struck. By then, the poor people relied too heavily on potatoes, so when the blight struck and the potato-crop failed, millions of our ancestors died of hunger. Those who survived soon got to know about how to properly grow potatoes and perhaps more importantly, also how to preserve them after they have been dug out of the ground.

The methods that worked were well understood in my day. Indeed it was a business in which the whole family took part. The first thing we did was chose the potatoes for sowing. We either used small, whole potatoes that showed signs of sprouting, or we took larger potatoes that had a number of 'eyes'showing, and then cut them up into 'slits'.

In my time growing up it was invariably the woman of the house who did this slitting. She selected one or two good top-eyes of the potato for each slit. In many cases two or more cuts could be obtained from each potato. The remainder of the potato (without top-eyes) was cut away and used for animal feed. The word we used to describe this remainder of the potato was a "laoawn". Each cut of potato contained enough substance to feed the new sprout until it sent out roots to gather its own sustinance from the soil. A potato smaller than a pullet's egg was considered too small to sow and would end up either on the dinner table or in the trough.

It is perhaps significant that the housewife took charge of the seed potatoes, as in those times she was also the housekeeper who provided food for the family. In our household slitting the potatoes was the only work that my mother did for the potato-growing. The site of where that crop was to be sown might be discussed, but such decisions were always made by my father.

The usual ground for growing potatoes was stubble-ground that had recently given a crop of oats, where the lea-land sods would be rotted by the time the potatoes started growing. This was the ideal ground for potatoes, but sometimes we might sow drills on a lea-land piece of ground, but this required an awful lot of harrowing to be done.

Sowing potatoes in ridges was the old-fashioned way in Ireland. The English ruling classes were often anxious to criticize the Irish for their stupidity, and used to refer to these ridges as "lazy–beds" which in fact, were something altogether different to raised ridges or drills. Ridges were simply long runs of raised land with furrows in-between. The farmer used a single-furrow horse-plough to pile up six field-lengths of furrows into a large ridge before moving into the second ridge. He did this until the whole field was ploughed into ridges. On farms where horse-power was not readily available, the farmer could hire a plougher to make these ridges while the farmer could be getting on with the work of sowing the seed potatoes and covering them with a spade and shovel.

The real 'lazy-beds' or as we called them "fodeens" were made in waterlogged land that was largely useless unless a lot of hard work was done. These lazy-beds were made by cutting three sides of a square sod with a spade before lifting and turning the sod back over on itself like a flap. You continued until you had a line of these sods turned over in a row. Then you stepped over and cut another row of squares on the far side, folding these sods in towards the others, thereby creating a ridge of paired, upside-down sods with a bit of space in between. You continued along like this, turning and folding each newly-cut sod until you had created long, flat ridges of upturned ground with strips of original grass or sedge down the middles, and with a dyke of at least two foot between each lazy-bed's ridge. Often, one man would work at least a half an acre in this fashion.

Now you had a uniformed ridge, consisting of paired sods turned inwards towards the middle with a strip of original ground between the upturned sods. You carted or carried farmyard manure or good soil or seaweed, or whatever other sort of organic material was available, and you spread this carefully on the top of the ridge, in between the turned sods. Next you dug out the furrows between the ridges to at least a foot deep, and broke this soil into a fine tilth and then you spread it carefully with the spade over the surface of the ridge. At this point you stuck down the potato seeds well out of reach of the crows.

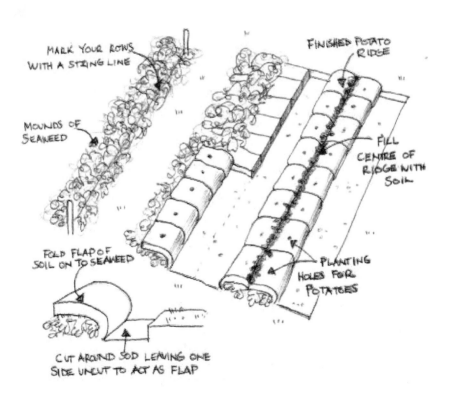

MARK YOUR ROWS WITH A STRING LINE

MOUNDS OF SEAWEED

FOLD FLAP OF SOIL ON TO SEAWEED

CUT AROUND SOD LEAVING ONE SIDE UNCUT TO ACT AS FLAP

FINISHED POTATO RIDGE

FILL CENTRE OF RIDGE WITH SOIL

PLANTING HOLES FOR POTATOES

Well-heeled visitors from the nearby island often spoke in a derisory fashion about the "ignorant and lazy Irish". But there was nothing 'lazy' about following the procedure I have just outlined. Turning near-useless bogland into crop-producing fields does not demonstrate any notion of laziness. In fact, having dykes or drains like this at four-foot spacings frequently drained all of the surface water, and the water that lay deeper underground could then be shored off to nearby drains. It was often that a farmer might decide to leave these dykes open for an extra year and then sow a crop of oats on these "fodeens" as was the description given to them in the old language. In this way, land that had never produced anything was brought into production through sheer hard work.

Sometimes a benevolent landlord would rent out such land—land which was of no use for grazing—to the very people who had been evicted off it, and who still resided in the locality. Recently, on a piece of wetland on which there was a very light covering of soil, I saw streaks of yellow ashes still lying close to the surface. This was a mark of some previous desperate efforts to farm there. This piece of land was a later addition to our original holding and was given to us by the Congested District Board in the year of 1907.

In this case, the land was so sterile that the whole of the covering of sedge had to be peeled off and cut into sods rather like turf. These sods were set up and dried in the March winds, before being burned in heaps, so that the ashes could then be spread over the ridges as fertiliser. I understand that a good crop of potatoes or oats could be squeezed out of this land in this fashion. But it could only be done once. It was hard, desperate, backbreaking labour and the families who did this work finally gave in. They walked to Ballaghaderreen and took the train to Dunlaoighaire, and thence to Hollyhead. For years, this family and their decendants have kept in touch with their old neighbours in Bruff.

The other 'modern way' of growing potatoes in my time was to make drills. By then, all of the hard work associated with potato-growing was done with the power of the horse. The only job that had to be done by hand was digging them up with a graipe – a four-pronged garden fork. One of the first jobs that I took part in as a man of fourteen years was digging out two drills alongside my father. I can still remember that pain in my back. The next year he decided to plough out the drills and then all one had to do was to pick up all of the potatoes to be seen and then sift through the soil with your fingers. It was a bit hard on the hands but it was a lot less detestiable than digging them out with a graipe.

One old-fashioned practice that we did hold on to, was covering the potatoes with scraws after they had been dug up. Scraws were a most versatile material for household repairs too. These scraws were cut off the surface of a level piece of ground. Experienced farmers would know at a glance the kind of ground that yielded good scraws. The blue sedge that grows on fairly dry bog—if it is on level ground—was usually selected. My father would go to the chosen site on a showery day (which was not suitable for doing major jobs) and would dig out sods no more than two inches in thickness and measuring approximately two-feet by two-feet-square. These would be stacked one on top of another like bulky tiles, up to about four or five-feet high. The idea was that they would dry out then, but not too much, because scraws that were too dry might crumble a bit. These scraws were cut carefully enough so that each fitted neatly against the other when laid out again. They were then placed over the potatoes like a carpet and, when slapped down with a spade would keep the potatoes dry and safe, at least until the heavy frosts expected from the middle of November.

Long ago scraws were also used as a kind of under-felt for roofing. Once the roofing timbers were in place – which were mostly wattles[1] that were harvested locally – these were then covered with a double layer of scraws. The thatch, which was usually made of rushes or straw was then laid over this, and scollops[2] were bent staple-like and driven deep into the scraws.

The roof was kept firmly in place, with the occupants inside as warm and snug underneath as tatties under scraws.

---

[1] *"Wattles" – a network of sticks or poles interlaced with twigs or branches.*
[2] *"Scollop" – a thin wooden rod or pin, used to secure thatch.*

21

Turf

FEW HOUSES IN the West of Ireland were far from the bog. If you stood outside our back door with a sling, you could land a stone in the bog, and this was the case in many a countryside house. However, all of the turf had long-since been cut away from these convenient bogs, and we had to travel about two miles for our turf. We had access to what was known as "turbery rights". In the late 1800's or early 1900's The Congested District Board acquired large areas of virgin bogs, and assigned about two acres of this bog to each local householder.

If you were lucky, you might get a piece of bog that yielded good turf and which was also sited close to a road. The best turf was located in the middle of the bog, which meant that the dried turf had to be transported across a soft and uneven surface. In those days this transportation was done by man, or beast, and the beast was usually a donkey, because a horse is a nervous animal who begins to plunge and thrash about if he feels himslef sinking. This usually ends with a dozen men or more, trying to pull him out. The donkey on the other hand is a more placid creature who is also much lighter, and so can often travel on a wet bog. Sometimes in an exceptionally-wet year, even the donkey cannot work on the bog, so the beast of burden is the man himself.

Turf varies greatly in quality, and not everybody is satisfied with the turf that he digs out of the earth. Some turf is known as "stone turf" and this is heavy and slow to dry, but it is also slow to burn and therefore gives out more heat. Another type of turf resembles a ball of your newspaper and it burns almost as quickly, but this kind of turf is easy to dry and does not break up. The breakage of turf is one of the biggest problems in turf-handling. If every sod that was cut in the bog actually reached the hearth stone in one piece, then turf-cutting could be reduced by about half. Turf cutting is especially tough work, and it behoves those who toil at such work to avoid breakagers at all costs, but we are not all sensible creatures.

The one great feature of working in the bog is the delightful enviornment. The wide expanse of purple heather and the peaceful surroundings, most especially in the early mornings. The warbling skylark rising up out of the heather goes on singing until he has gone out of sight in the clear blue sky. The butterflies with their magic colours just flicking about in a leisurely fashion, and then the buzzing honey bees – all business. Soon enough, the peaceful scene is invaded by noisy people who seem to have planned to all arrive together – for maximum effect. Their braying donkeys coughing out different tunes, while blue-green smoke lingers along the ground as if reluctant to go upwards and soil the clear sky. Most people liked to light a fire when they arrived, and would set the kettle on top so that the prospect of a hot mug of tea helped, 'to soothe the savage breast'. Some are grumbling while others break into song. Soon,all is silent again, as the work begins. A whole lot of digging has to be done before even one sod of turf is cut.

Approximately four feet of the bank is cleared of heather and surface material, to a depth of about six inches. This part of the operation is done with a normal spade and shovel. To prepare the section of bank for cutting, a line of sods of triangular shape are first cut out with the spade. Then the inner edge of the section is deeply scored with a spade so as to separate it from the main bank, and now the turf cutting proper, begins.

The sleán is specially designed for turf-cutting. It is a small, light, long-handled spade, with a wing on one side of the blade to help fire the cut slices of turf up and aside. If an able-bodied man is available, the cutter of the turf slings the turf off the sleán into the air and this able-bodied man deftly catches these sods and builds them carefully on a turf-barrow. The turf barrow resembles more of a small cart than a barrow. Some called it a 'bog barrow'. It has two strong shafts for pulling or pushing and a high front end with no sides. The main feature of the turf-barrow is that the single wheel is about four inches wide. This is to ensure that the wheel can ride on the soft uneven terrain of the bog without sinking. In this operation, the wet, freshly cut turf can then be transported to good drying ground.

My own experience of turfcutting on my own, was that I would sling the sodden turf off the sleán clear in front of me so that the sods stayed intact, and then slid off the sleán cleanly without breaking. When the bank was cut to the end of the section the spreader began where the turfcutter left off, and could pick up the cut sods in layers, without much breakage. This took considerable skill and practice. I have often heard derisory comments about turfcutters being men of low intelligence. I doubt if anyone who has cut turf would subscribe to this comment.

The turf needs many a twist and turn before it is dry enough to transport home, and be fit to use on the fire. After the turf has been lying on the ground for a few weeks it needs to be put standing on one end – each sod resting against the next one, so as to drain the

moisture out. If the weather is good and if the quality of the turf is good' and if the drying ground is not too damp, this might be all that is necessary before the next operation of transporting the turf from the middle of the bog to the roadside. Seldom do all of these drying conditions occur though, so there may be a second handling of the turf before it is fit to transport out.

Turf Barrow

Turfcutting had to be done during harvesting and haymaking seasons. This was another problem for the busy farmer,

116

because the fine day that might have been spent transporting the turf might have to be spent bringing in the hay or spraying the potatoes. People who had no other business except looking after the turf used to feel that they were busy enough. I recall a man who would pass us on the road on his bicycle, and he'd salute my father in the following terms.

"Very good weather for the turf!"

Or as appropriate. .

"Very bad weather for the turf!"

It happened that my father was busy thinning the sugar beet and he was thinking of the hay and the spraying and the bog. Turf was well down on his list of priorities, but often there was a valley period between the time that the hay was finished, and before the harvest was ripe. At such times work on the turf could be fitted in. Carting home the turf was often left until the harvest was in, provided the pile of turf on the roadside was stacked up in such a way that it would not get too wet in the autumn rains.

It seemed that every hour of every working day was slotted for some job. Work on the farm was rarely done of a Sunday. I never knew of any ordinary farmer to take a holiday away from the farm. The only interuption was a death in the family, and this took two days. These were the only holidays allowed.

22

Bruff

A PICTURE OF THAT rolling countryside is printed on my mind. I know the bounderies of each holding for miles around. We had six fields that were arable. The biggest field we had was five acres and the smallest field had exactly one acre that was arable. There was a well at the lower end of most of our fields, as most of them were sloping in some direction. There was a skirt around these wells that grew sedge and rushes. On the higher ends of our fields the soil was light and the limestone gravel was close to the surface. This meant that water that fell as rain quickly soaked down through to the gravel and then the water flowed along the sub-soil and came back to the surface at the lower ends.

It was a relatively easy matter to catch this water and channel it in a stone drain into one of the open ditches at the field boundaries. The arable fields comprised only about half the total area of our holding. The remainder was an open wild area where the cow and the horse and the ass had free range for the whole of the year. Some natural vegetation was produced in this area, and it seemed sufficient to ensure that the animals did not become obese. Father used to describe this part of his holding as "the exercising ground".

In the early 1830's my great Grandfather Micki Coen, walked down the four miles from Knock to have a look at the place in Bruff. He met the occupier, one Mr Thomas Burke, who was sheltering in the only one barn that had a roof. He had no animals on the farm and he was depending on wild fruits and berries, and was catching wild birds for food. There was no other person residing or depending on the farm. Mr Burke was more than glad to accept the extra Five Pounds that Micki gave him for the "good will" of the deal. With money in his pocket Mr Burke set off for Liverpool, and the very next day Micki and his wife Biddy McNicholas – along with their two infant sons – took posession of Bruff. The deal with Mr Burke seems to have been a most amicable one, for when Micki's sons grew up and went away they would meet up with Thomas Burke at his home in England, and he was always anxious to meet them and to learn about all of the old neighbours at home.

A threshing-barn was the first building that Micki made habitable. He had been living with Biddy and their sons in Flatley's threshing-barn in Knock before he made the move to Bruff. It appears that in those times, a threshing-barn was often made available to couples who had no other accommodation. Later, when Micki got on his feet so to speak, he often made his own barn available to others in need of accommodation.

There was a prohibition by the Landlord from removing bog deal from the nearby bog. 'Bog deal' were stumps and roots and branches buried in the bog - the remains of ancient forests which had lain undiscovered until the turfcutting era began, and you could often come across great clusters of them. Micki used some of this wood to carry out some minor repairs on the other outbuildings, and when he saw how the wind was blowing, so to speak, he began to lift some good long bauks of bog deal. He may have done this work under cover of darkness, I do not know. But my father who knew no Irish was able to quote the following;

"Ta se Cam Patch. " – "It is crooked Pat."

"Seo uaith an tua." – "Here is the axe."

Bog Deal

Later, his sons and grandsons would roof houses with shop timbers. This required more accuracy and precision so they took father's references to the axe and the bog-deal as a joke. But they marvelled all the same, at how Micki had

119

somehow repaired all of the farm buildings and had constructed a reasonably-good dwelling house at little or no cost, except hard work. In the meantime his family had grown to six; three sons and three daughters.

He was doing this work throughout the years when the great famine was at its peak. His daughter used to boast that they had never tasted any of the "Yellow Buck" by which euphemism she was referring to the maize-meal or so-called 'Indian porrige' served up to the Irish poor during the famine.

When I was very young we visited a grand old lady who lived in the nearest house to ours. She had spent years in America, and she loved to talk about her young days in Ireland before she had gone to America. She had grown up with my Grandfather and his family and she loved to tell us about the old people and their ways. It is to her we owe most of the information about Micki and his wife Biddy. They were both thrifty people, and sometimes they behaved in odd ways that were not fully understood or approved of by their offspring. One odd trait that Biddy had, was to light the lantern at midnight after all were asleep, to bring out a special mash for the hens. The neighbours used to be talking amongst themselves and wondering if Biddy was 'alright upstairs'?

Her husband too had some odd ways. Instead of chatting with the neighbours, he grew 'quare plants' up in Garraidh Ard, where he spent most of his evenings. The sort of stuff that he grew up in the garden, sure, you couldn't eat the likes of it, "Suf go deo!"[1] Was their response.

"You'd been better with a few praties, when we had them."

But somehow, Biddy and Mikki's children grew big and strong, and never went hungry. One explanation for Micki's 'odd ways' was that he had worked in the County of Waterford, and it was there that he had learned these curiousities. The story we heard, was that Micki had been going to a hedge-school somewhere in the vicinity of Knock and, in an effort to continue his education he had travelled to County Waterford where an order of monks that had been routed

---

[1] *(Loose translation) - referring to something disgusting.*

out of France at the time of the Revolution, were developing a farm. These clergymen had first taken a place in Rathmore Co. Kerry. This was not to their satisfaction, and then they got an offer of some ground in Erris, Co Mayo. This, according to the Prior, had too much turf underneath, and so would not be suitable for farming.

Their agricultiral explorations eventually brought them to the Commeragh Mountains in Co Waterford. There, they decided to settle. Local Parish Priests assisted their brethern from France by sending them young Irishmen to dig out the surface of the mountainside. There, they sifted-out and unearthed large stones and used them to build the boundary-walls.

Recently I spoke to the present Prior. He is an old man, walking with aid of a stick, with about three other fellow-priests who are as feeble and decrepit as himself. There are no young priests in that monastery any more. They used to keep records of all of the leaders of their pious group, but they did not bother to keep records of the men who did the hard digging. Later, they built a magnicent college and a Church and Priory. This school provided education for those who could afford it from Waterford and the surrounding counties. There was, however, no record of Micki, nor of any of his hardworking colleagues.

The long green fields rising high into the hills, and the straight stone walls and the canal that to this day flows from the mountain past the Priory, is testiment to the industry and the skill of these labourers. I could see the fine farm buildings and the creamery-tanker used to bring milk from the monastery to the local creamery.

The inspiration these visitors from France brought to the area, is still evident today. The water from their stone canal, generated electricity long before it was in any of the local towns. Micki picked up a few ideas from them too. Flat stones are not available aroud Bruff, but Micki used local round stones instead to build underground drains, and over one hundred and fifty years later these drains still work, and are shoving out water at Bruff.

It is hard to gauge how much education Micki picked up in his travels. Irish was his first language at home. My uncle Pat spent his early days with his grandparents Micki and Biddy, and told me that he never spoke a word in English until he went to the local school in Doogarry. Micki named all of his fields in Irish. They are Glas na nairne (green sloes), An Pairc Ban (white field), Pairc mhor (big field), Cruckan col (hill of the h a z e l - tree), Garraidh Bhille (Billy's field), and the Sraith (damp field). His favourite was Garraidh ard (high garden). I do not know whether or not he could also read and write in Irish.

He could certainly speak English, and could read and write in it as well! His expertise was much in demand in the locality mainly for writing out petitions. These petitions were usually to the Landlords for time to pay the rent, or for some other . It appears also that litigation was fairly common in those days. Micki would listen to the story of the plaintif or the respondent, and then write out the account in English so that the Magistrates could understand. These fine and noble gentlemen had taken a solemn oath before God to adminsiter justice to all of the people of the land, "equally, fairly and without fear or favour"- but they never even went to the trouble of understanding the spoken or written word in Irish.

End.

The Author Joe Coen

Born in 1937 in Aghamore in County Mayo, Joe Coen grew up in rural Mayo. He had the usual experiences of young people of his time. He attended the local primary school until he reached the school leaving age of fourteen. From that time onwards he worked on his father's farm.

Joe did every job on the farm except shearing sheep. In one respect he outdid DeValera who claimed that he did every job on the land except ploughing. Joe became a ploughman at fifteen years of age and he ploughed with a team of horses for four or five years. He was also an experienced bog worker. He saved turf and cut it with the old fashioned slean. He was well used to driving a donkey in the rough soft bogs.

He finished full time education when he was fourteen years of age, but he became an avid reader; a reader of whatever he could lay his hands on. Books were not plentiful in his household nor were they available to him locally. At the age of eighteen he got a job with the ESB. A year later he went to work in England. He returned home and helped to build a family dwelling house.

At the age of twenty one years he applied for and was admitted as a member of An Garda Síochána. While working in Kildare he

became aware of the second hand book shops on the Quays in Dublin. No visit to Dublin was complete without a few second hand books. These were mainly old text books on English and Irish language. He claims now that he could easily fill a good sized car trailer with books that are supposed to be good for him. The possession of all these books is just evidence that he had good intentions. It is not evidence that he has read them all.

Joe worked as a Garda in Counties Carlow and Kildare and also Cavan and Leitrim, and then in 1967 he came to Co Roscommon as a Sergeant and he retired as a Sergeant in Roscommon town in 1990. He married Betty in 1966 and they had five children. Betty died in 2010, and now Joe lives lonely and alone in Roscommon.

(Left) Joe and Betty, (above) Joe with siblings Tess and Bill and their parents Nora and Willie.

In his retirement years, Joe has taken to jotting down his memories of old Mayo. You can find his other popular books, "Two Dry Sods" and "The Man About Town" by searching online.

Printed by BoD™in Norderstedt, Germany